THE RESPECTFUL SCHOOL

HOW EDUCATORS AND STUDENTS CAN CONQUER HATE AND HARASSMENT

STEPHEN L. WESSLER

WITH CONTRIBUTING AUTHOR WILLIAM PREBLE

ASCD

Alexandria, Virginia USA

1703 N. Beauregard St. • Alexandria, VA 22311-1714 USA
Telephone: 800-933-2723 or 703-578-9600 • Fax: 703-575-5400
Web site: http://www.ascd.org • E-mail: member@ascd.org
Author guidelines: www.ascd.org/write

Gene R. Carter, *Executive Director*; Nancy Modrak, *Director of Publishing*; Julie Houtz, *Director of Book Editing & Production*; Tim Sniffin, *Project Manager*; Reece Quiñones, *Graphic Designer*; Keith Demmons, *Typesetter*; Dina Seamon, *Production Coordinator*.

Printed in the United States of America.

ISBN-10: 0-87120-783-4   ASCD product no.: 103006
ISBN-13: 978-0-87120-783-8
Also available as an e-book through ebrary, netLibrary, and many online booksellers (see Books in Print for the ISBNs).

Library of Congress Cataloging-in-Publication Data
Wessler, Stephen.
  The respectful school : how educators and students can conquer hate and harassment / Stephen Wessler with contributing author William Preble.
     p. cm.
Includes bibliographical references and index.
  ISBN 0-87120-783-4 (alk. paper)
  1. School violence–United States–Prevention. 2. Bullying in schools–United States–Prevention. 3. School environment–United States. I. Preble, William, 1953- II. Title.

  LB3013.3.W47 2003
  371.7'82--dc21
                                    2003009003

13 12 11 10   12 11 10 9 8 7 6

In recognition of the far too many girls and boys and young women and young men whose school years are dominated by fear and anxiety caused by bias, prejudice, harassment, and violence.

In memory of those students who, because they saw no way out of a school life filled with despair and anguish from constant harassment, took their own lives.

For Nate and Seth, from whom I learned more about the courage of students to stand up to bigotry and prejudice than from anyone else.

For Becca and Maya, in the hope that their school years will be joyous, fulfilling, and free of bias and hate.

For Beth, who has patiently provided me with support, encouragement, and love during my years prosecuting and working to prevent hate crimes.

The RESPECTFUL SCHOOL

How Educators and Students Can Conquer Hate and Harassment

ACKNOWLEDGMENTS

This book reflects the hard work, creativity, and thoughts of my colleague Bill Preble. His contributions in cowriting the Introduction and Chapters 1 and 7, based on his innovative work in evaluating school climate and peer leader programs, are invaluable.

I am indebted to my closest and oldest friend, Bruno Anthony, who provided his expertise in child psychology to cowrite Chapter 8.

Tyler Christensen worked long and hard to develop the valuable Appendix to this book, detailing additional resources for educators.

Karen Pushard patiently and expertly typed and retyped the many drafts of this book.

Peggy Moss provided a valuable and thoughtful substantive edit of the manuscript.

This book has benefited, beyond my ability to describe, from the careful and insightful work and encouragement of my editor, Bob Cole.

Finally, this book would not have been written were it not for the years of collaboration with a wonderful, talented, and committed educator, advocate, and friend, Betsy Sweet.

INTRODUCTION

A few years ago, I received a telephone call from a principal of a middle school participating in the State of Maine Attorney General's Civil Rights Team Project, a peer leader program focused on the prevention of hate crimes. At that time, I was the prosecutor in charge of civil rights enforcement for the attorney general's office. The principal called to tell me a "remarkable" story involving two brothers who were students in the adjoining high school. These boys came from a very poor family. They came to school in old clothes, sometimes with patches and other obvious repairs, and always out of fashion. The brothers were quiet, not very popular, and the butt of continual jokes, put-downs, and snide remarks from a group of four or five other high school boys. The remarks began every morning when the brothers got on their school bus and never let up until they got off to go to their first-period class. Every afternoon when the brothers left school, the humiliating process repeated itself.

One boy who rode the same bus, a middle school student, became increasingly upset about the mean and degrading treatment of the two brothers by the older high school students. Two mornings before the principal called me, this boy decided to do something. The Civil Rights Team at his middle school had a suggestion box that students could use to send the team information about things of concern. The boy wrote a short anonymous note explaining that he rode Bus No. 6 and was upset about how these two brothers were treated. He added that he was too scared of the "tough" high school boys to say anything to them. When the 12 student members of the middle school Civil Rights Team opened their suggestion box that same day, they read this note and immediately passed it on to their principal. The principal read the letter and sent a copy of it to the bus company. The next morning, just as school began, a man in his late 40s knocked on the principal's door and asked if he could speak with her. He explained that he was the driver of Bus No. 6 and that his supervisor had given him the student's note that morning. He told the principal that he had no idea that this harassment was occurring on his bus and that he was very sorry. He abruptly turned around and left.

The next morning two things happened. First, when Bus No. 6 was going up the long drive to the combined high school-middle school building, the driver stopped the bus 200 feet from the front door. He walked to the middle of the bus and began to tell the students about his experience as a child from a very poor family, and how students in his school constantly made fun of him because of how he dressed, how he smelled, and what his parents did for work. He said that although 25 years had passed, he could still remember those comments—every one of them. He then looked at the group of high school boys who sat behind the two brothers and said in a low but intense voice that from this morning on "no one—not one single student"—on his bus would make fun of or humiliate anyone else. Without ever mentioning the two brothers, the driver walked back to his seat and drove up to the school.

Later that same morning one of the middle school students on the Civil Rights Team came into the principal's office and asked if she would give a letter to the two brothers. The student explained that the team did not know the brothers' names so they hoped that she could deliver it. The principal took the letter and told the student that she would give it to the high school principal to pass on to the brothers. The letter started "Dear Brothers" and expressed how sorry the team was that they had been made fun of and that these middle school students hoped that people would be "nicer" to them. The middle school principal gave the letter to the high school principal, who handed it to the two brothers later that morning.

It is difficult to imagine what that morning must have been like for the two brothers. They started their day, like every other day, expecting to be humiliated for who they were and who their parents were. And then suddenly their bus driver spoke and the harassment ended for that day, for the rest of the week, and for the remainder of the year. In addition, they received a letter from 12 younger boys and girls who told them that other students did care about them and how they had been treated.

*   *   *

This book is about bias, prejudice, harassment, and violence between students in our schools. It is about the power of words to hurt and wound—and to heal. Most important, this book is about solutions—what educators and students can do to create and to maintain a climate of respect and civility in our schools so that no child walks through the hallways and sits in the classrooms feeling scared.

Core Beliefs

Our approach to preventing school bias, harassment, and violence rests on the following core beliefs:

- Every child has the right to be physically and emotionally safe at school.
- Children cannot learn and cannot grow to their fullest potential when they fear for their safety.
- It is possible to create schools and classrooms where a climate of safety and respect enables all children to thrive and succeed.

If educators are to develop *effective* strategies for preventing bias, harassment, and violence, they must reflect on, select, and then act on their own core values and beliefs. These values and beliefs are the foundation on which we can change language and behavior and create a climate that allows students to learn without fear.

The Problem

I'm in special ed, and when people call me stupid every day, day in and day out, after a while, you just can't stand it anymore.

There is one girl on the bus who is pretty fat. The other kids pick on her so bad, every day. I don't know how she can stand it.

I was harassed daily about being gay or bisexual, and it got so bad that I attempted suicide.

A group of boys ganged up on one girl, calling her a "whore" and a "slut" till she dropped out.

Someone etched "KKK" on a desk that a black 11th grade girl sat at every morning. She was very scared and started missing school.

In recently completed studies of student perceptions of the social and academic climate within 36 schools in Maine and New Hampshire, William Preble and others (2001) noted the following observations from students about their schools:

• Aggressive, uninterrupted verbal abuse happens to many students every day.

• Schools are full of injustice toward certain students who are viewed by peers as being "different."

• One in five students does not feel safe at school.

• Some students leave school every day frustrated and angry because of their mistreatment by peers and, in some cases, adults in the school.

The problems of harassment and bullying have been well documented by others as well (see Centers for Disease Control and Prevention, 2001; American Association of University Women Educational Foundation, 2001; Human Rights Watch, 2001; Shively, McDevitt, Cronin, & Balboni, 2002; and Bureau of Justice Statistics & National Center for Education Statistics, 2002).

As disturbing as this information is, the problem does not end with the widespread use of degrading language and the frustration and anger that such language leaves in its wake. Too many students have their school experience defined by fear—fear of the next humiliating comment or fear of the potential for violence that is inherent in so much verbal harassment. And finally, too many of our students are the victims of violence that all too frequently results as degrading words escalate to stronger degrading words to threats and finally to blows.

Creating Respectful and Civil Schools

We can create schools in which *all* children feel respected and valued, schools in which no children sit in class fearful and anxious about what might be said or done to them as they walk through the hallway to their next class. Schools must take two critical steps to create this kind of environment. First, teachers, staff, and administrators must *give voice* to civility and respect. Second, schools must provide student leaders with the skills and confidence to stand up and speak out for their classmates who are the victims of harassment and humiliation.

Giving Voice to Civility

Adults can, and must, give voice to civility and respect in many and varied ways. Administrators must create antiharassment policies that are clear and fair and then must explain those policies to the entire school community. Administrators must speak to the entire school community—faculty, students, and parents—and explain in firm and resonating words that bias and harassment have no place in the halls, classrooms, cafeterias, or playing fields of our schools. Administrators must respond in visible ways when a serious incident of bias, prejudice, harassment, or violence occurs—ways that are visible not only to the perpetrators, but also to the victims, the student body, and the faculty and staff.

Teachers and staff must also speak up by responding immediately, consistently, and firmly when students engage in harassing conduct or use degrading language or slurs. Teachers and staff must intervene when they hear these words used not only in the classroom but also in the halls, in the cafeteria, or on the playing fields.

Student Leadership

Providing students who are viewed as leaders and role models by their peers with the knowledge, empathy, and skills to speak up for respect is an essential component of any comprehensive strategy to change school climate and to reduce harassment and violence. Adults cannot change school climate by themselves. Students are also powerful role models. When harassment and violence occur in school, students are always present, but teachers and administrators often are not. When we affirm the fact that the courage and empathy of students are a valued asset within a school, when we recognize that students are not the source of the problem of bias, prejudice, harassment, and violence but rather the source of the solution, we send an empowering message of dignity and respect to our young people.

When student leaders step forward and speak out to stop the routine use of put-downs and slurs, their actions resonate. When student leaders assume responsibility for making our schools safe for everyone, they model empathy and courage and encourage other students to do the same. When speaking up for respect becomes "cool" and becomes the norm, the school climate can change. Bringing students from all social and academic groups within a school to work together to solve the problems of bias, harassment, and violence is a powerful strategy for creating safe schools. (For more information, see "Peer Leadership: Helping Youth Become Change Agents in Their Schools and Communities" at the Web site www.partnersagainsthate.org.)

We Can Do Better

When degrading comments, harassment, and disrespect are widespread, a school climate can develop that leads to increased violence, self-destructive behavior, suicide, dropping out, and academic failure. We adults must take a hard look at the social and learning climate that exists within our schools. But studying school climate is not enough. We must take what has been shown to work most effectively in changing the climate of disrespect and intolerance and implement these ideas and practices in schools everywhere.

The bias, prejudice, harassment, and violence in our schools create an educational system in which our core beliefs sadly are unrealized. Instead, we find that too many students go to school in fear for their physical and emotional safety, and too many students are denied the opportunity to learn and grow to their full potential because they focus their energies on trying to keep safe.

This situation should not be and, most important, does not have to exist. We can change the social and educational climate of our schools by developing comprehensive and coordinated strategies that empower the adults in our schools to stand up for civility, that value the classroom abilities and contributions of every student, and that nurture the leadership abilities of our children.

Sadly, the story of the two brothers who began every school day by being humiliated and degraded is not unusual. The middle school students and the bus driver who changed the lives of those two brothers by speaking up for respect need not be part of a rare success story pitted against the constancy of harassment. Students, bus drivers, teachers, principals, and communities can make schools safe for every student.

But getting to this point requires investing in the resources and the time to provide the members of our school communities with the knowledge, the skills, and the confidence to speak up for respect. The return on this investment can change entire institutions. It can also create a climate where two brothers can begin their day in school feeling valued, confident, and ready to learn.

The Scope of This Book

Part I of this book covers the dynamics and impact of bias, harassment, and violence. To begin, Chapter 1 discusses the extent of use of degrading language and slurs by students, as well as the process of escalation from the routine use of disparaging words to violence. Chapter 2 examines what happens when escalation runs its course and violence erupts: how violence manifests itself in schools and whether we can successfully deter the perpetrators from repeat behavior. Chapter 3 probes the emotional impact of bias, prejudice, and harassment on children who are targeted.

Part II focuses on how we can create respectful schools. Chapter 4 discusses the importance of teachers' intervention when students use degrading words, as well as providing guidance for intervening in different situations. Chapter 5 covers the approaches we can take to address the needs of victimized students. Chapter 6 examines the many ways in which administrators can lead their schools toward a climate of respect, including the development of effective antiharassment policies and the response to violent incidents. Chapter 7 focuses on the critical role that student leaders can play in creating respectful and civil schools. Chapter 8 considers the ways we can respond to acts of terror affecting not only our nation but also our schools. Finally, Chapter 9 celebrates the power and courage of our students who stand up for each other.

References

American Association of University Women Educational Foundation. (2001). *Hostile hallways: Bullying, teasing, and sexual harassment in school.* New York: Harris Interactive.

Bureau of Justice Statistics & National Center for Education Statistics. (2002). Prevalence of students being bullied at school. In *Indicators of school crime and safety, 2002.* Washington, DC: National Center for Education Statistics & Bureau of Justice Statistics. Available at www.ojp.usdoj.gov and http://nces.ed.gov/pubs2003/schoolcrime/index.asp.

Centers for Disease Control and Prevention. (2001). School health guidelines to prevent injuries and violence. *Morbidlity and Mortality Report, 50*(RR-22), 16–17.

Human Rights Watch. (2001). *Hatred in the hallways: Violence and discrimination against lesbian, gay, bisexual, transgender students in U.S. schools.* New York: Human Rights Watch.

Preble, W., Langdon, S., Taylor, L., & Ashton, K. (2001). *Maine civil rights team evaluation.* Augusta, ME: Office of the Maine Attorney General and Maine Justice Assistance Council (copublished report).

Shively, M., McDevitt, J., Cronin, S., & Balboni, J. (2002). *Understanding the prevalence and characteristics of bias crime in Massachusetts high schools.* Boston: Northeastern University.

PART I

THE DESTRUCTIVE POWER OF BIAS, HARASSMENT, AND VIOLENCE

1

FROM WORDS TO VIOLENCE

The use of degrading language by students is both pervasive and destructive. Disparaging words are destructive for two reasons: they create a climate in which words can escalate to violence, and they create debilitating emotional trauma for the boys and girls who are targeted. One of educators' most important tasks in addressing the destructive power of words is getting students to understand that slurs and put-downs are widespread and are a powerful force for creating incivility, disrespect, and violence.

A few years ago during a two-week period, I gave about two addresses a day to middle and high school students in suburban and rural communities on the impact of verbal harassment and the importance of students' taking stands to prevent harassment. Toward the end of the two weeks, I became increasingly tired of giving the same address time and time again. In my last address, on impulse, I began by asking all of the students in the high school to raise their hand if they believed that their school had a serious problem with students bringing dangerous weapons to school on a daily basis and using those weapons daily. Not surprisingly, no hands were raised. I let 10 seconds go by in silence before I raised my hand. I told the students that I thought that they were wrong in their assessment and that dangerous weapons were brought into and used in their school on a regular basis. Those weapons were words—put-downs, slurs, and degrading language. I went on to describe the pattern of escalation in which verbal harassment leads to stronger and more focused harassment, which leads to threats and, possibly, violence.

Later in that same address, again on impulse, I asked all the students to raise their hands if that morning in school (they had been in school for only an hour and a half before I began my address) they had heard another student use a degrading word about girls or women. Ninety percent of the students raised their hands. I then asked the same question with respect to degrading comments about gays or lesbians, no matter how the comment was intended. Again, 90 percent raised their hands. In speech after speech in middle schools, high schools, and colleges over the past several years, I have used a similar approach and have received similar responses. Part of the process of beginning to focus on addressing harassment is to develop an understanding throughout the school community that demeaning and degrading words are harmful and that their use is pervasive, if not endemic, throughout the school.

Pervasiveness

Students in middle school, high school, and even college consistently report that verbal harassment based on physical appearance, sexual orientation, academic ability, physical and mental disability, socioeconomic status, gender, religion, race, and ethnicity is pervasive. Although many students do not use degrading language and slurs, every student hears these words many times a day on the school bus, in the hallways, in the cafeteria, in the locker rooms, and on the front steps of the school itself.

I have found that students use these words in two fundamental ways. The most frequent use of slurs, put-downs, and degrading language is by students who have no intent to hurt or wound anyone else. Rather, these students simply are using a word that they have heard and perhaps used for years. Sometimes these words even assume new meanings to the speakers. For example, middle school and high school boys often use the six-letter antigay word beginning with *F* as a synonym for "jerk." Highly charged and sexually degrading language, antigay words, and other words denigrating particular groups are thrown around the hallways of our schools with abandon and without much thought.

The second way in which these words are used is far more intentional and mean-spirited. A small number of students use denigrating language in a purposeful way to hurt or wound a particular target.

Students tell me that the use of the words in the first way is most common. Students hear degrading comments about girls and women, gays and lesbians, persons with disabilities, persons of color, and persons from non-Christian religions multiple times per day. These words have become the background noise of school hallways. Students also tell me that the second way in which the words are used is far less frequent but still pervasive. Specifically, students report hearing mean-spirited, targeted, and bias-motivated comments about particular students from a couple of times a day to a couple of times a week. And, of course, some students say they do not hear these mean-spirited comments at all.

Beeper Studies

For the past several years William Preble has been collecting data on the nature and extent of harassment in middle and high schools. His research has been based on a three-pronged approach involving in-depth interviews of students, schoolwide surveys, and "beeper studies."

Preble learned about beeper studies by reviewing the work done at the University of Chicago by Mihaly Csikszentmihalyi and his associates in their study entitled *Being Adolescent* (1984). Preble modified the original design slightly for his school-climate research in New England. Students who were interviewed were asked to participate in the beeper study portion of the research process. These students were trained to carry and use electronic pagers (beepers) and to document their observations of school life whenever they were silently beeped (the beepers were set on "vibrate"). The beepers were set off six to eight times a day over the course of three or four days. When students were paged, they carefully observed the things going on around them for a five-minute period. When signaled by a second page, they wrote down what they had observed on an observation form. The process generated hundreds of real-time snapshots of life within schools and offered a student's firsthand view of school climate.

Preble's work in one New Hampshire school district with two middle schools and one regional high school provides a disturbing picture of the extent of verbal harassment, as indicated by the following conclusions:

• The vast majority of students in these three schools experienced or observed routine verbal harassment for the ways they or other students looked and dressed.

• Between 50 and 75 percent of all students at the high school and just slightly fewer in the two middle schools personally experienced more disturbing forms of harassment related to being gay, unintelligent, or disabled, or witnessed such harassment being directed toward others.

• Twenty-five percent of students experienced or witnessed verbal harassment related to family income, religion, race, and gender.

• The frequency of the harassment grew steadily each year from middle school through the senior year of high school.

• The most dramatic increases in the levels of verbal harassment from middle school to high school happened in some of the most potentially explosive areas: harassment based on religion, race, and gender.

Where Students Learn Degrading Words

Students learn degrading words and slurs from at least three sources. First, some, but certainly not all, students hear these words from their parents. When I have called parents of middle school and high school students who have been involved in hate crimes, I sometimes have learned within the first seconds of the conversation where the students learned their messages of bias and prejudice; the parents were unable to refrain from using that language in their conversation with me. However, in many other instances, parents of young hate-crime perpetrators have broken down in tears and bewilderment as to how their child could have engaged in such destructive conduct in a home where diversity is valued and degrading language is not used. Second, young people learn the language of degradation and bias from popular culture. Radio, movies, television, and popular music at times use language containing slurs and degrading language to catch the attention of and entertain their audiences. Both of these sources, parents and popular culture, are important because they send an implicit message that disrespectful words are acceptable.

But equally important is the third source: other young people. Whether they hear these words from older brothers and sisters or on the school bus when they first start going to school, students are bombarded with what eventually becomes a background noise of degradation and put-downs. Many of us can remember the first time we sent our son or daughter to school on the bus. Sometime in that first week or two, our children began using slurs that were never used in our homes. The role modeling by other students is a very powerful influence.

Whatever the source and whether or not students are using degrading words casually without any intent to hurt, the language of degradation and hate has the capacity to escalate from words to threats and, finally, to physical assaults. This belief that words can be used as dangerous weapons—that words are part of the process of escalation from language to violence—is supported both by my experience in investigating and prosecuting hate crimes and by research by Preble and others (2001).

Escalation

Toward the end of one school year, when I was directing the Civil Rights Unit in the Office of the Maine Attorney General, we filed a case in court involving bias-motivated violence and threats among students. The events, however, did not begin in the late spring. Rather, they had begun in early January immediately after students returned from the December break. Four boys began targeting another boy named John with antigay slurs. When the boys first began to use slurs about John, they did not say them to his face. Rather, they said the words to themselves and to other students. Some of their friends laughed, some of them joined in, but none of the students spoke up and said, "Stop talking about him like that." After about a week the four boys got the idea that what they were doing was "okay," and they took it to the next level. They began to say the slurs directly to John, almost always in front of other students. And again they received the same response from their friends and classmates. Some students laughed, some joined in, some were quiet, but none spoke up.

After another week to 10 days of verbal harassment directed at John, the four boys took it to the next level. When John was walking down the hall, one of the students would walk behind him while another would walk beside him. The student walking beside John would put his foot out, and the student walking behind would push him over. John would tumble to the floor, books falling, while the boys yelled the same antigay slurs. Again, their friends and classmates who saw these ugly incidents said and did nothing to stop the harassment.

In the beginning of February, the boys took the harassment to a far more serious level. In two separate incidents during that month, the boys jumped John somewhere in the school during the school day. One of them put him in a headlock while the others punched him in the stomach and kneed him in the groin, all the while yelling antigay slurs. Again, students saw this conduct and no one spoke up or reported it to teachers or administrators.

Between the beginning of March and the first week in April, three more serious incidents occurred. However, the constant verbal harassment and the tripping and pushing continued throughout this period almost as background noise. Moreover, up until the last incident in this sad string of events, no member of the faculty, staff, or administration was aware of anything that was going on. In the first week in March, three of the boys jumped John in the boys' bathroom and, while yelling antigay slurs, tried to push John's head into an unflushed toilet. John struggled and was able to escape before suffering that indignity. A couple of weeks later John was walking in school during the school day when one of the boys came up behind him and put a noose over his neck. This was not a piece of string but a sturdy rope, tied as a noose and pulled tight enough that it took John 35 to 40 seconds of struggling to get it off his neck and over his head.

A week later, in early April, the boy who had put the noose over John's head came up to John and told him that he knew where his father kept his handgun and that he was planning to bring it to school the next day and shoot John, shoot John's supposed gay boyfriend, and then shoot himself in the head. A student who overheard this comment immediately told a teacher, who told the principal, who called the local police department, who called me at the Attorney General's Office. When we investigated this case, we learned two significant facts. First, the boys involved were all 12 years old, 7th graders at a K–8 school. Second, and most important to an understanding of the impact of verbal harassment, was the escalation took place over four months from the use of

degrading language and slurs in early January to life-threatening violence and threats in April. *In every single hate-crime investigation I
conducted in a school environment, whether in a middle school, a high
school, or a college, I saw that same pattern of escalation from the routine use of degrading language and slurs to stronger degrading language,
to threats, and to violence.* The cases I investigated never started with
the punch or the threat but invariably began days, weeks, months,
and sometimes even an entire school year earlier with the routine,
and often unthinking, use of demeaning and degrading words—
words that no one interrupted.

Research focusing on violence in middle and high schools confirms the anecdotal data that I compiled in years of hate-crime
enforcement in schools and colleges. In a study published in 1997 by
the U.S. Department of Justice, Daniel Lockwood analyzed violence
in middle and high schools and found that "[i]n the largest propor-
tion of violent incidents, the 'opening move' involved a relatively
minor affront [usually involving 'minor slights and teasing'] but *escalated* from there" (p. 2, emphasis added). Moreover, other students
who were present only rarely intervened to try to avoid the escalation from verbal harassment to violence.

Understanding the process of escalation is critical to understanding why I refer to degrading words as dangerous weapons, but
it is even more critical to understanding the importance of intervening consistently to interrupt the use of those words by boys and
girls in our schools. I have seen this escalation with every type of
harassment. For example, if boys in a high school routinely use
highly charged, sexually degrading slurs about girls—not directed at
any particular girl but just as words that to them do not have much
meaning—it should come as no surprise that when those words are
not interrupted and challenged, some boy will get the idea that it is
OK to direct those same words toward a particular girl or young
woman. And when no one challenges the propriety of speaking in

that way, it should come as no surprise that some boy will get the idea that it is permissible to say those same words in anger to a particular girl or young woman. And when no one interrupts those words of anger, no one should be surprised that some boy takes it to the next step and gropes a girl in a hallway. And finally, when one month, two months, three months later we learn that a girl has been the victim of a date rape in the back of a car or at a party, no one should be surprised at all.

Escalation usually occurs over a period of days, weeks, or even longer. But the process also can occur far more quickly—sometimes even within minutes. One example involved a 9th grade girl who had moved from New York City to a small city in Maine over the Christmas recess. On the bus on the way to her second day at her new school, a much larger 11th grade boy looked at her and yelled a racial slur. Not one student reacted. So the boy stood up and, while pointing at the girl, yelled the same slur and the words "Go back to where you came from." Again, no one said anything. The boy continued and told the girl that she had moved into his neighborhood and that he was going to burn her house down one night while she and her family were sleeping. The entire incident took less than 90 seconds.

When students use degrading words, put-downs, and slurs without anyone taking notice, a very disturbing and ultimately very destructive message is sent to a broader group of students: namely, that the use of that kind of language is not wrong. Sadly, in far too many instances, the result is the creation of a climate in which students believe that it is acceptable to take harassment to its next level.

It is important that we understand the dynamics of that next level: the violence that too often erupts in hallways, on buses, and outside school buildings. Understanding these dynamics will improve our ability to structure responses that can keep our schools respectful and safe.

References

Csikszentmihalyi, M., & Larson, R. (1984). *Being adolescent: Conflict and growth in the teenage years.* New York: Basic Books.

Lockwood, D. (1997). Violence among middle school and high school students: Analysis and implications for prevention. Washington, DC: National Institute for Justice. Available at www.ncjrs.org/txtfiles/166363.txt.

Preble, W., Langdon, S., Taylor, L., & Ashton, K. (2001). *Maine civil rights team evaluation.* Augusta, ME: Office of the Maine Attorney General and Maine Justice Assistance Council (copublished report).

2

THE DYNAMICS OF SCHOOL VIOLENCE

Too many people view school violence as encompassing only a small range of serious criminal conduct. The U.S. Surgeon General's 2001 report on youth violence limited its focus to serious violence, defined as murder, attempted murder, aggravated assault, and rape. These are the categories of violence that make the evening news and the morning papers. Other types of violence tend to be ignored or labeled as constituting only harassment and bullying.

School violence, however, does include far more than serious felonies. John, the middle school student whose sad experiences are described in Chapter 1, certainly was the victim of violence when his classmates put him in a headlock, punched him in the stomach, and kneed him in the groin. Certainly he was the victim of violence when a classmate slipped a noose over his neck and pulled it tight. But the escalation from verbal harassment to violence occurred earlier. When John was shoved into lockers, tripped, and pushed to the floor of the school hallway and verbally threatened, he also was the victim of violence.

Shoving a student into a locker or a wall is a misdemeanor and is violent. Threatening to beat up a classmate is a misdemeanor and is violent. As the next chapter makes clear, the emotional impacts of misdemeanor assaults and threats, and even of noncriminal verbal harassment, can be as devastating to children as the impact of serious violent crimes.

A school in which students slam classmates into walls or lockers, stuff students into lockers or toilets, and threaten to beat up children who are perceived as different is not only a school with a harassment problem, but also a school with a violence problem. By broadening our definition of school violence, we accomplish three things. First, we recognize the real and traumatic experience of students who are assaulted and threatened. Second, we conform our definition of violence to the provisions of criminal law. Finally, by dispelling the illusion that assaults and threats are only forms of harassment, we can mobilize faculty, administrators, school boards, parents, police, and students to work together to prevent violence.

Equal Opportunity Violence

In the early 1990s, when I was asked to create a hate-crime enforcement unit within the Office of the Maine Attorney General, I knew that a significant portion of hate crimes were committed by teenagers and often occurred in school. When I began prosecuting hate crimes in schools, I assumed that I would find one group of students who targeted black students, another group who targeted gay and lesbian students, another who targeted Jewish students, and on and on. I quickly learned that for the perpetrators of violence, those distinct groups of victims did not exist. Instead I found students who could switch with disturbing ease and rapidity from targeting Asian students on Monday to disabled students on Tuesday to gay or lesbian students on Wednesday. Their biases and their animosities were not directed at only one group. They encompassed all groups that were different from themselves and that were small in number within the school population.

Several years ago, I worked with a police department to investigate what appeared to be a "routine" case of school vandalism. Someone had broken into a middle school at night and scratched hate graffiti onto desks, lab tables, and blackboards. The messages were both racist and anti-Semitic. The only unusual aspect of the report from the principal was that someone also had taken a 25-gallon drum of formaldehyde from the biology lab.

The next day a 16-year-old boy named "Sam" met with the police to talk about his friend "Michael," also 16. Sam said that he had broken into the school with Michael and that he had decided to talk to the police because he was scared. He was scared because Michael made bombs. Sam explained that Michael had begun a couple of years ago with pipe bombs that he used to blow up small animals. Michael was now experimenting with timing devices.

On the basis of that and other information, the police obtained a warrant to search the home Michael shared with his parents. They found a basement workshop with metal pipes, electronic timing devices, various explosive materials, and the 25-gallon drum of formaldehyde. In Michael's bedroom they found books on bomb making. Above his bed were a picture of the Unabomber and a one-page sheet with instructions for making a bomb with dehydrated formaldehyde.

Later that day I met with Sam in an interview room at the police station. Sam said that he became scared when Michael said he only would use bombs against people he did not like. I asked Sam whom Michael disliked. Sam responded slowly, "Michael really dislikes blacks." He paused and added, "But he can't stand Hispanics, and he really hates Jews." Sam paused again. "But he hates gays even more." After a final pause he said, "I think he hates the Chinese more than anyone." At first I thought that Sam was being a smart aleck. Then I realized that he was merely taking his time to remember Micheal's comments about whom he disliked.

Although the breadth of Michael's biases is disturbing, it is not unusual. I have seen case after case in which young people aimed their anger and violence at individuals who were different from the majority without much thought as to why they were different.

Equally important, I have seen this same phenomenon with students who engage in nonviolent verbal harassment. Those students who use degrading language toward gay or lesbian students also tend to use sexually degrading slurs toward girls or racist comments toward students of color. Students who use put-downs toward disabled students also tend to demean students who do not wear the "right" clothes or who are overweight.

Following the Pack

Several years ago, my office prosecuted a case involving a sophomore boy who was walking home from his suburban high school on a Friday afternoon in mid-September. The boy was thought to be gay by many of his classmates. As he was crossing a busy street, he saw 11 boys from his grade. One of the boys yelled out one sentence: "Let's get the . . . " followed by an antigay slur. With nothing more to incite them, all 11 boys began chasing their classmate across the street while yelling the slur. They quickly caught up with him, surrounded him, and continued yelling slurs, which soon were interlaced with threats of violence. When they started hitting the boy, he fell to the ground and rolled into a fetal position. His classmates then began kicking him with full swings of their legs, first into his side and then into his head. Finally, one of his classmates pulled from his left pocket a bandana and from his right pocket a padlock. He tied the bandana to the padlock, swung it three or four times, and finally whipped it into the boy's left elbow. The next day when I received a copy of the police report of the incident, the hospital report was attached. I was unable to understand the technical language used by the emergency room physician to describe the injury to the elbow, so I called him up. I will always remember the words he used to describe the boy's injuries because the words were so unusual. The physician said that the elbow had "imploded—everything that had been attached was now unattached."

When we investigated what lay behind this attack, we found that none of the boys knew their gay classmate very well, none had any personal animosity toward him, and none but one had a history of deeply held and vehement antigay views. What occurred on those suburban streets was the same "following the pack" phenomenon that I have seen in one physical attack after another both in and outside of schools. It appeared that one sophomore was the leader of the group, and when he yelled "Let's get the . . . ," his 10 classmates, with adrenaline pumping and without any thought, took off in pursuit.

The need for peer approval and the fear of standing up to friends are so powerful that students with no history of violence can join in vicious attacks with apparent ease. Professors Jack Levin and Jack McDevitt of Northeastern University, in their study of the motivations of perpetrators of bias crimes (2002), found that many young hate-crime offenders acted spontaneously for a "thrill" rather than out of any deeply held commitment to bias and prejudice.

I also have observed the same follow-the-pack phenomenon with nonviolent verbal harassment in school hallways and cafeterias. Students feel intense peer pressure to join in bias-motivated harassment and bullying. Students who are upset by verbal harassment directed at others often remain silent bystanders both because they have no role models for intervening and because they fear that if they speak up they will become the next target for harassment.

Deterring the Perpetrators of School Violence

The Civil Rights Unit that I directed enforced a hate crime law that authorized the state attorney general to obtain injunctions or restraining orders against the perpetrators of hate crimes. A growing number of states have similar laws. These restraining orders prohibit perpetrators from committing any future bias-motivated violence, threats, or property damage aimed either at the particular victim they had targeted or anyone else.

These restraining orders are similar to those obtained by women who have been the victims of domestic violence. Many people believe that restraining orders in domestic violence cases work some of the time but are more often flagrantly violated. However, my experience with hate crime injunctions, particularly with teenagers, is very different from the experience with injunctions against men who beat their spouses or girlfriends. In seven years of enforcement beginning in the early 1990s, only one teenager subject to a restraining order was found to have engaged in a second bias-motivated incident, a rate of recidivism that is close to zero.

Why are these restraining orders so effective in stopping young bias-crime offenders from repeat incidents? Some suggest that the fear of criminal prosecution for violating these orders is the reason that repeat behavior happens so infrequently. But domestic violence orders also are backed up by a threat of criminal prosecution. Rather, I believe that the effectiveness of these orders is related to the peer pressure that leads so many teenagers to join in bias-motivated violence in the first place.

The boys and girls and the young men and women who commit bias-motivated violence believe their classmates will view them as heroes and heroines when they return to school. They believe this because they hear slurs and degrading language all the time in their schools and rarely hear any students speak up to express their disapproval. They believe that their friends not only share their biases but also approve of the violence that they used to act on those biases. But their whole belief system is turned upside down when police charge them with a hate crime.

When the local newspaper condemns hate violence on its editorial page, when clergy sermonize against bias and prejudice from the pulpit, when administrators, faculty, and staff express their disapproval, these young men and women begin to doubt their status as heroes and heroines. But most important, when these young hate crime offenders learn that their friends and classmates are disgusted by what they have done, they realize with a stark clarity that they are as far from being heroes and heroines as possible. Suddenly, the bragging rights disappear, the peer pressure shifts, and these young men and women realize that bias-motivated violence is a ticket to nothing but trouble and ostracism. As a result, recidivism is almost nonexistent.

References

Department of Health and Human Services. (2001). *Youth violence: A report of the surgeon general.* Washington, DC: Department of Health and Human Services.

Levin, J., & McDevitt, J. (2002). For the thrill of it: The strong preying on the weak. In *Hate crimes revisited: America's war against those who are different.* Boulder, CO: Westview Press.

3

THE EMOTIONAL IMPACT OF BIAS, PREJUDICE, AND HARASSMENT

The pattern of escalation from words to violence described in Chapter 1 certainly has tremendous potential for harm. But words of prejudice, degrading comments, slurs, and unkind jokes have the power to create even more damage. Sadly, some children cannot even envision living in a world without the oppressive weight of verbal harassment. Here is how one teenager described his fantasy of a place without harassment (Center for Educational Media and Center for the Prevention of Hate Violence, 2001):

> My fantasy is that people will be able to get along and not do these stupid things that aggravate people and harass people. And one of my fantasies is going to heaven because I believe that when I get there I won't have to worry about all this harassment. . . . I just won't have pain, and no one will be going through pain. I look forward to it because it will be like the better place than this world.

For children like this boy, who could envision no earthly alternative to the constant harassment he was forced to endure, the emotional and physical impacts of bias and harassment are both intense and damaging. Indeed, some children are so adversely affected by verbal harassment that they lose their opportunity to play, learn, and enjoy life. Instead, these boys and girls and young men and women are compelled to focus their attention upon far darker and destructive emotions.

When I first began investigating hate crimes, I noticed a phenomenon that repeated itself case after case, year after year—with both young people and adults. The victims of violent hate crimes—people who continued to suffer significant physical ailments days, weeks, and even months after a violent attack—did not want to talk about their broken bones or their concussions. They wanted to talk only about the words that were used against them.

I particularly recall a case in which two men, one in his mid-40s and the other in his early 20s, were having an intense conversation in a booth at a local diner. Two larger men seated across the aisle began to make degrading antigay comments directed at the two men involved in their intense conversation. The two diners tried to ignore the comments even though the harassment persisted throughout their meal. When the two men finished their meal, they paid their bill and started to leave the restaurant. As they were walking outside, they were brutally attacked from behind by the larger men. The older man's glasses were broken, and he received several hard blows to the face and head. The attackers yelled antigay slurs and then ran.

Several weeks later, after the attackers were identified and court action was initiated, I interviewed the older of the two victims in preparation for trial. It was important to obtain a precise account of his physical injuries and their lingering effects so that we could present that information to the court. The man briefly explained that he was still having headaches and blurry vision and that both were interfering with his ability to pursue his work as a commercial fisherman. As I began to ask more detailed questions about his physical condition, the man became more and more frustrated. He kept on interrupting me to say that he did not want to talk about the physical effects of the attack. Finally, he stood up and said, "Stop asking me about my physical problems. I want to talk about what is important to me. I want to talk about how I could be having dinner with my son, whom I had not seen in four years, and how those men could say those disgusting words just because they thought we were gay. I want to talk about how much worse it must be for gay men in America to go through life knowing that they can be degraded and attacked at any time. It's simply not right." Time and again I learned from victims of hate crimes that their concussions and blurry vision usually healed, but the lingering scars from the words of hate lasted much longer—and for some never completely went away.

Fear

The most prominent emotional impact of words of hate is fear. If there is one common failure that law enforcement officials, health care professionals, and educators typically share when working with victims of bias, prejudice, and harassment, it is the failure to understand how the use of "mere" words can create a range of emotions from mild anxiety to paralyzing terror.

Many of us find it hard to understand how the use of a single demeaning word can create fear. Most of us have experience with words that make us irritated, angry, embarrassed, and ashamed, but seldom can we fully understand the intense fear that words of hatred can produce. Unfortunately, students of color, Jewish students, Muslim students, girls, gay/lesbian/bisexual/transgender students, students with disabilities, and others understand this impact with a crystalline clarity.

Several winters ago Maine experienced what became known as "The Ice Storm." The ice storm was a freak meteorological event. What started as rain in the warmer upper atmosphere turned into ice as it descended, landing on tree limbs and power lines. Over seemingly endless hours of freezing rain, more than two inches of heavy ice coated many branches. The weight on trees and power lines finally went beyond the point of tolerance. The night of the ice storm in my rural home was unforgettable. Every 30 to 45 seconds we heard what sounded like a cannon shot that was actually an entire tree, a large branch, or a power line snapping under the accumulated weight of the ice. I was unable to sleep that night because of the constant anticipation of the next "shot of the cannon"—a crash that might bring a limb or an entire tree down on the roof of our house.

In the months following the ice storm, I heard several high school students in different parts of the state refer to themselves as the "ice storm kids." These students, however, were not referring to their experience living through the night of the ice storm. Rather, they were using the phrase to describe their everyday experience as students in their schools walking down the hall. For them, the constant anxiety of waiting for the next degrading comment or slur that would make their stomach feel like it was ready to drop to their feet, or the next push or shove into a locker, was the same anxiety that many of us felt through that awful winter storm. The saddest thing that I heard from these boys and girls was their relief when, walking through the halls of their school, they heard the degrading slurs or felt the shove into a locker. They were relieved, they told me, because they felt that once the indignity had occurred it would be unlikely to happen a second time during their walk to their next classroom. It is extraordinarily difficult to focus on algebra when you are spending your class time in fear and anxiety about the walk through the halls from algebra to history class. This is no way to experience school; this is no way to experience childhood.

In school after school I hear that boys and young men routinely, and often without malice, use highly charged, sexually degrading language about girls. These boys generally do not think much about these words. For them, they are nothing other than words that they hear constantly in the hallways, on the buses, and in the locker rooms. The problem, however, is that these words are never *just words* to girls or young women who six months, six weeks, or even six days before had heard those words said by a man in their bedroom or in the back of a car as they were raped or otherwise sexually assaulted on what they considered the worst night of their lives. For these girls and young women, the casual use in school of those highly charged, sexually degrading words can bring back consciously or unconsciously those awful moments of a sexual attack and turn even a safe school into one that seems filled with menace and the potential for violence.

For many students the use of the language of hate is so inextricably interconnected with a history of violence that hearing the words themselves can create fear of that violence. To black students who have sat around the kitchen table listening to a grandparent tell stories of lynchings in the South, to Jewish students who have heard stories of relatives who did not make it out of concentration camps in Eastern Europe, to gay and lesbian students who know of friends who were severely beaten, the language of bias and prejudice is rarely "just words," and the fear that those words can create is often extraordinarily intense.

Several weeks after the attack on the gay sophomore by 11 classmates described in Chapter 2, when the case was close to being resolved in court, the prosecutor whom I had assigned to the case came into my office at the end of the day looking pale. She said that she had just finished a conversation with the mother of the student who had been attacked. The prosecutor asked the mother how her son was doing, and the mother responded that although her son's elbow was mending, he was not doing well at all. The mother explained that she and her husband had just found out that their son had spent the last two weeks sleeping on the roof of their house. The prosecutor in my office said, "Ma'am, I do not believe I understood you correctly. Could you please repeat that?" The mother quickly responded, "No, you heard me correctly alright. Our son was so scared that his classmates would find a ladder and climb into his second-story bedroom window and kill him in his sleep that he found a flat part of the roof over the den and took a cotton blanket to try and sleep." In Maine in mid-October, a cotton blanket is not warm enough to allow anyone to sleep, much less stay focused the next day on algebra and history. The fear and terror created by bias, harassment, and hate are intense and sometimes intolerable.

Anger

On March 5, 2001, a high school boy named Andy walked into his San Diego-area school with a 20-caliber revolver and opened fire in the boys' bathroom and then in the hallway, killing 2, wounding 13, and firing 30 rounds in all. As Andy's story unfolded in the days following this tragic attack, the nation learned from his friends that he had been picked on, teased, and harassed constantly. And how was Andy harassed? With words. Andy, however, moved beyond the anxiety and fear and turned instead to anger. In Andy's case, the anger exploded into bullets, blood, and bodies in the halls of his school.

The United States has seen such highly publicized, multivictim school shootings only rarely. A far more common image is the student who has been on the receiving end of slurs month after month, who moves beyond fear and turns to anger, and then punches the face of the last student to utter a slur. All too frequently, the student who resorts to violence against a harasser finds himself in serious trouble under the school disciplinary policy—and perhaps under the juvenile criminal process. Physical violence is a serious violation of school policy and may constitute a crime. The student who yelled the slur, however, might serve, at most, an in-school detention.

It is nearly impossible for school administrators to resolve this situation in a way that lets not only the student who struck the blow but many others feel that equity and justice have been dispensed. I have found that many students who are victims of verbal harassment secretly wish that they had hit the boys or girls who tormented them with degrading comments. This larger group of students, along with the student who now finds himself suspended or facing prosecution for assault, may see a world in which the victim, and not the perpetrator of harassment, is punished.

Denial

A colleague of mine often refers to the boys and girls who are targeted with bias, prejudice, harassment, and even violence as the "stealth kids," after the high-tech bomber that is able to get in *under the radar*. For many adolescents, getting in under the radar screen, not calling attention to yourself, not broadcasting your problems, is a goal in and of itself. However, for students who are targeted with bias, prejudice, harassment, and violence, the impetus to stay under the radar often leads to a denial that they are being targeted at all. I remember a Jewish boy, a high school junior, who was standing on the athletic fields after school watching the track team practice. Another boy, who had been harassing the Jewish student with anti-Semitic slurs for some time, came up to him and yelled that the Jewish boy should be put into a gas chamber like the other Jews, and then he punched the Jewish boy in the eye. The aggressor was quickly taken to the principal's office. The Jewish student, however, disappeared for more than an hour. When he finally resurfaced and was interviewed by the principal and asked why the other boy had hit him, he replied, "I wasn't hit." Not only was the boy sporting a black eye that could have come out of the makeup room in a Hollywood studio, but also the entire incident was observed and heard by two coaches and a dozen students. This boy's desire to "get in under the radar" led him to deny what was obviously true.

Why do the targets of degrading slurs and harassment refuse to report these incidents to teachers or administrators and sometimes even deny that incidents have occurred? Two reasons help explain this phenomenon: (1) fear of retaliation and (2) fear of a situation known as "secondary victimization."

Retaliation

Students who are subjects of bias and harassment frequently believe for two distinct reasons that things will get worse if they report harassment. First, many students believe that schools will not be able to protect them from retaliation by their harassers. Specifically, these students believe that if they report harassment, their tormentors will respond by targeting them for increased harassment and possibly violence. Second, many victims of harassment believe that once the larger student body learns of the harassment, as a result of incidents being reported to teachers or administrators, more and more students will join in. This problem is particularly poignant for students who are gay/lesbian/bisexual/transgender/questioning, or who are straight but mistakenly targeted as gay or lesbian. These students may fear, with justification, that if they disclose to an adult in the school that they are on the receiving end of antigay harassment, the harassment will spread from one or two tormentors to a much larger group of students.

I have found that the risk of retaliation is significantly reduced when faculty and administrators demonstrate they are committed to preventing harassment and violence by responding promptly and appropriately through the school's disciplinary system. The students who engage in harassment and violence almost invariably are engaged in cowardly acts of intimidation. When schools respond in a comprehensive and forceful way, those students generally focus on their own problems rather than on retaliation.

Secondary Victimization

Secondary victimization is a term used by professionals who work with victims to describe a situation that occurs when authorities or others in the community minimize the victim's experience, either by not seeming to care, by explaining that there are more serious issues to deal with, or by suggesting that the victim should stand up for himself or herself and "take care" of the problem. To students who are suffering intense fear and anxiety from harassment but have been told by administrators, teachers, or coaches that their problem is not serious or that they should take care of it themselves, the message they receive is to keep their problems to themselves. These students suffer isolation and loneliness that are both terrible and terrifying. Sadly, and sometimes tragically, the failure of students to report harassment allows harassment to continue and possibly escalate to serious violence or to cause greater and greater damage to the victim's already bruised emotions.

Loss of Spirit—and More

Some students suffer more than fear, anger, and denial from harassment. Some students also lose their spirit. I find that the young people who suffer most from prejudice and harassment are not those who experience fear or even physical violence. I find that most students eventually get over their fear and anger, broken bones and concussions usually heal, and rage usually subsides. However, those students who lose their sense of spirit, their sense of hope, and their sense of faith in the goodness of others often lose something with far more lasting effects.

Several years ago on a Friday afternoon in the early fall, I received a call from an elementary school principal who told me of the experience of a new 4th grade student named April. April was black, the adopted daughter of two white parents. April was the only black student in the school. Within the first week of school, on the bus, a classmate of April's began asking her pointed and mean-spirited questions about her physical appearance. Soon she began making more explicit, racially derogatory comments. At about the two-week point in the school year, this classmate handed April a drawing of a black girl on a scaffold with a noose around her neck. Underneath the scaffold was April's name, and underneath her name, a racist slur.

I reached April's mother by telephone in the early evening on the Sunday after my conversation with the principal. She told me about the incident, and then I asked her how her daughter was doing. She responded that a half an hour before I called, April had come up to her and said, "Mommy, I wish I was white."

The depth of the loss of spirit and hope that would cause a little girl to want to change such an essential part of who she was is both disturbing and sad. Unfortunately, too many children who face unrelenting and seemingly unending harassment feel that the only way to end the harassment is to change into someone other than who they are. Many, however, cannot change, and instead experience a deadening of their spirit. Some of these children, however, lose even more.

Loss of Education

Students who are targeted for harassment, who are anxious and scared, who are angry, who have lost their sense of spirit and joy, often find they are unable to focus on schoolwork. These students become less able to focus and pay attention, which results in lower grades and declining satisfaction from their academic experience. Sadly, some students who are the victims of harassment lose their education entirely by dropping out of school.

I have heard account after account of high school students who felt so discouraged, so alone, and so without hope of avoiding degradation, humiliation, and fear that their only recourse was to sacrifice their opportunity for a diploma. Somewhat surprisingly, I have heard the same story from college students. Recently, a college sophomore told me about a gay classmate who during their freshman year was the victim of repeated slurs and jokes that escalated to death threats. The sophomore said that she lost contact with the gay student at the end of their first year in school. When she started her sophomore year, she did not see her classmate but assumed that he was living across campus and taking different courses than hers. One afternoon she stopped at a music store on the other side of the city from the college and ran into the gay student. He explained that he had left school because of the harassment and threats, had lost his financial aid package, and did not think he would be able to return to college—ever.

Loss of Health

Students who are targeted with harassment suffer physical and emotional effects ranging from sleeplessness, anxiety, and depression to weight loss or weight gain. Some students turn to self-destructive behaviors including alcohol and drug abuse.

I have spoken to far too many students whose health dramatically deteriorated during middle and high school because of the harassment they were forced to endure. Although some of these students obtained help from health care and mental health professionals, many did not. These students not only endured continued harassment but also experienced the anxiety and depression in silence.

Loss of Life

Some boys and girls and young men and women who are continually harassed in their middle and high schools lose it all and take their lives. Although the number of these suicides is small, even one teenager who dies because he or she sees no escape from unremitting and unrelenting harassment is one too many.

Recently I conducted an orientation program for the first-year class at a college. I addressed the entire class of incoming students on the impact of harassment. Following the address, the students broke into small groups, facilitated by older students, and discussed their experiences with harassment and, most important, what students could do to make their college as safe and respectful a place as possible. Finally, the students came back together for a wrap-up session.

I began the wrap-up session by asking students if they had seen the impact of harassment at their high schools. The first student to speak, nervously holding a portable microphone, related a story of a girl in her high school class who attempted suicide after enduring months of verbal harassment and threats. Each of the next four students talked about a friend they had lost to suicide. In each instance the victims had been targeted with unrelenting harassment.

We Can Do Better

We may never be able to protect *every* student from the deep emotional trauma inflicted by harassment. But we know that we can do better; we know that we can dramatically reduce the number of students whose school experience is defined by fear or anger or hopelessness. We can make fundamental changes in school climate by investing the resources, the energy, and the time to provide our teachers, our administrators, and our students with the knowledge and the skills to make our schools as safe as possible.

The chapters in Part II explain how we can make that change happen. Specifically, they address the following questions:

• How can teachers intervene effectively to halt bias-motivated harassment?

• How can administrators develop comprehensive antiharassment policies that are understood by faculty and students?

• How can administrators respond to serious incidents of harassment or violence in ways that energize the school community to create safe and respectful learning environments?

• How can faculty and administrators respond sensitively to the needs of children who are the victims of harassment?

• How can schools create peer leader programs that empower students to stand up for each other?

• How can schools respond proactively to the fear and prejudice created in the wake of terrorist attacks?

Reference

Center for Educational Media and Center for the Prevention of Hate Violence (2001). *Violence: It Starts wth Words.* South Portland, ME: Maine Department of Corrections and Southern Maine Technical College.

PART II

CREATING CHANGE IN THE SCHOOL CLIMATE

4

THE IMPORTANCE OF TEACHER INTERVENTION

Recently I talked with two middle school boys about students' use of degrading language and slurs in their school. They said that students used degrading words toward girls and toward gays and lesbians "all of the time." They added that racist and anti-Semitic language was used on a regular basis, but less frequently. A short time later, I also talked to one of the teachers in that school (let's call her Ms. Smith). I asked her whether the school had a problem with students engaging in verbal harassment of traditionally targeted groups. She told me that she never heard such language either in her class or in the hallways.

The next day I spoke to the same two boys and told them that I was confused. I reminded them of our prior conversation and then told them that I had spoken with Ms. Smith and that she did not hear the kind of slurs or put-downs that they had described. Almost in unison, both boys said, in slightly different words, "Oh, nobody would use those words in front of Ms. Smith." What became apparent in further conversation with the two boys was that Ms. Smith, in effect, created a moving zone of civility as she walked through the hallways and conducted her classes. She was known as a teacher who always intervened to interrupt the use of put-downs, slurs, teasing, and harassment. It is ironic, but in my experience not unusual, that Ms. Smith, who was so effective in stopping harassment in her presence, was unaware of the prevalence of degrading language elsewhere in the school.

Most students I talk to know a teacher like Ms. Smith. But sadly, these same students tell me that they know a large number of teachers, staff, and administrators who, in their view, hear degrading language, slurs, and put-downs as they walk through the halls or in the cafeteria, but these adults fail to react at all. In fact, approximately one-third of the high school and middle school students surveyed by William Preble in Maine and New Hampshire schools told us that when faculty, staff, and administrators hear students using degrading language and slurs, they do not intervene.

When students believe that an adult heard degrading and uncivil language but failed to speak up, the effect is powerful and disillusioning. Most students understand from an early age that other students will use put-downs and engage in teasing and harassment. Students, however, expect that the adults in their schools will speak up to create an atmosphere of respect. The students who are most devastated by slurs and put-downs are those who believe that an adult whom they both care about and look up to heard the comments and did nothing. These students often interpret the silence of teachers as condoning the slur or put-down.

Students sometimes are mistaken that a teacher has actually heard degrading comments. However, the implicit, unintended message sent to students who engage in harassing conduct is equally damaging if teachers do fail to react. Students construe the silence as implicit permission to continue verbal harassment. As a consequence, some of these boys and girls do continue their harassment and, over time, engage in increasingly disruptive and violent behavior.

What Kind of Intervention Works?

The same kind of intervention does not work equally well in every situation. In the hallway or in the classroom, the most effective intervention will vary depending upon a number of factors, including whether the degrading language was used "routinely" without any intended target, whether the comment was used to intimidate a specific student, and whether other students heard the comment. However, every effective intervention has common elements: *timeliness, consistency, firmness,* and *respectfulness.* Effective intervention by teachers can successfully change the conduct by reducing the use of degrading language, can make targeted students believe that someone cares about their concerns (as well as bystanders who feel that the words are about them—even if no one else knows), and can provide powerful models for students to speak up when they hear slurs and put-downs.

Timeliness

Faculty should respond immediately to the use of degrading comments and put-downs for several reasons. First, interventions will have the greatest impact when students have a clear memory of the words. Second, when faculty delay speaking to a student, other students who heard the comment likely will not be present to hear the faculty member's response. Consequently, those other students may believe that the teacher did not care about the comment or even that the teacher condoned its use. Third, an opportunity delayed may well turn into an opportunity lost. Faculty who plan to speak to students "later" may forget about the incident, may be unable to find the student, or may lose the impetus to speak up.

Consistency

When faculty consistently intervene to interrupt students' use of degrading language, they set a standard for acceptable conduct in the school. On the other hand, when faculty members intervene only occasionally, they send a mixed and confusing message: degrading comments and put-downs are unacceptable some of the time but are not so bad at other times. Consistency, however, does not demand perfection. It is very difficult for most of us to respond *every single time* we hear harassing and disrespectful comments. Sometimes we have not fully heard the comment; other times we are distracted; and in other situations we just do not have the energy to say anything. Being consistent requires being vigilant and pushing ourselves to speak up for a civil and respectful atmosphere; but consistency takes into consideration human nature—none of us is perfect.

Firmness

The use of degrading language is a serious problem in our schools and deserves a serious and firm response. When faculty members respond to slurs and put-downs in a joking or lighthearted way, they send a confusing message. Students may wonder whether the faculty member really was disturbed by the language or was only going through the motions of intervening.

Respectfulness

When faculty intervene to respond to the use of slurs and disparaging comments, they model for students the courage and confidence to speak up for a safe school environment. But faculty also create a role model for students by *how* they intervene. It is important for several reasons that the intervening adult treats the student who used a slur respectfully. First, an intervention that embarrasses or humiliates a student is more likely to make the student angry or resentful than encourage the student to seriously evaluate his or her conduct. Second, many students who use slurs do not intend to do anything disrespectful or hurtful. Rather, they are simply using a word that they hear others use all the time. When faculty suggest through their response that the student was acting in a purposefully mean-spirited way, the student may feel unjustly criticized and become both defensive and resistant to change. Finally, other students watch *what* faculty members do and *how* they do it. If adults in the school intervene respectfully, students will do the same.

Intervening in Different Situations and Contexts

In the Hallway

Teachers often wonder how they should respond when they are walking through the hallways and hear a student use a slur that is not seemingly directed toward any particular student. Teachers tell me that in this situation they often do not know the names of the students involved or even which student in a group actually made the comment. My answer starts with what *not* to do. This is not the time to call the SWAT team from the local police department. Nor in most schools (depending on the disciplinary policy) is this the occasion to send the offending student to the principal's office. In many schools, the principal's office would have to be moved to the gym if every student who used degrading words was sent to "the office." Rather, this situation calls for the faculty member to send an immediate and clear message that he or she heard the comment and that the language used is not acceptable.

The use of "I" statements can be very effective. Comments such as "I do not appreciate that kind of language" or "That word offends me" send a clear message that you find the language unacceptable.

Some teachers use shorthand comments of one, two, or three words: "Watch your language!" "Language, please!" or "I heard that." A group of 50 faculty members might have 50 different and equally effective ways to send a message that adults in the school do not accept the casual use of degrading language.

What all of these responses have in common is that they are timely, consistent, firm, respectful, and *brief*. When you are walking to your next class you do not have the time to hold a 30-minute,

10-minute, or often even 2-minute discussion of the negative consequences of the use of slurs and put-downs. Each of the suggested comments requires only seconds to say.

In the Classroom

The routine use of slurs in the classroom presents different issues. For example, if a student makes a casual derogatory reference about Jews to a student sitting next to him, a teacher needs to decide whether to say something immediately to the entire class or wait until after class to speak privately to the student who made the comment. I believe it is critical to respond immediately to the student who used the slur and to make the comment audible to the entire class. However, it is important to recognize that the student may not have meant to do anything hurtful or destructive. Rather, the student may simply be repeating language used by family members or friends. Consequently, the teacher's response should not embarrass the student or suggest that the student is a heartless bigot.

It is effective to explain that the words the student used are demeaning to Jews. It is critically important to send the message that the use of degrading words about Jews or any other group is not acceptable to you in your class or anywhere else.

I believe it is important for faculty to discuss the issue in front of the entire class because other students likely have heard the anti-Semitic comment. Most of those students, however, will not hear a private conversation between the teacher and only one student at the end of the class. Students who are upset about the anti-Semitic comment may assume that the teacher did not care. Students who use similar derogatory language may assume that the teacher condones the use of put-downs and slurs because they have not heard the teacher respond.

Finally, this situation allows teachers to take advantage of the "teachable moment" and to address the general use of degrading language (or, specifically, the use of anti-Semitic comments) in more detail either as part of the class curriculum or as a stand-alone exercise. The Appendix provides a list of organizations and Web sites that faculty can refer to for help in developing and integrating materials relating to bias and harassment into their instruction.

During a Class Discussion

Not long ago I received a phone call from a high school principal who wanted advice on how to handle a situation that had arisen in a social studies class. The class was discussing World War II and the Holocaust when a boy said, "My father is a member of the Nazi Party, and I think Hitler was a great man." The teacher immediately sent the student out of the classroom and directly to the principal's office.

This situation differs from the use of degrading comments or slurs in the hallway or even in the back of a classroom. As upsetting as the student's views are, he was expressing his opinion on a topic being discussed in class. I suggested that the student's statement might be protected under the First Amendment to the United States Constitution. I also suggested that the teacher could address the situation not by curtailing the student's comments, but by engaging herself and the entire class in *more discussion* about the Holocaust and Hitler's role in the death of millions of Jews and others. I further suggested that the teacher could let the class know that she—as well as countless world leaders, religious leaders, and scholars—condemns Hitler and the abominable acts that he and others committed during his years in power. I provided the principal with the contact information for organizations that have developed curricula on teaching about the Holocaust (see Appendix). Finally, I suggested that the teacher meet privately with any Jewish student in the class and any other students who appeared to be upset by their classmate's comments.

Hurtful Words "Taken Back"

During faculty inservice workshops in high schools, teachers frequently raise a difficult issue: handling a situation in which black students, gay students, young women, or students from other traditionally targeted groups use words that are usually considered to be slurs toward their own group in talking to each other. The issue is complicated by the concept of "taking back a word." Individuals and groups who have been targeted with bias, prejudice, harassment, and violence may begin to use between themselves the very words that previously had been used by others to humiliate and denigrate their group. They may do this to defuse the negative and degrading power of the word when used by others. What complicates this question even further is that the process of "taking back a word" may actually change the meaning of the word itself. What may be a harsh slur when used by someone who is not gay or someone who is not black may evolve into a word of pride or friendship when used by students within a particular group.

I recently presented a workshop to a group of college students from around the country on issues of bias, prejudice, and harassment. When the issue of groups taking back words came up, a black student from a university in the Southwest told us about a pickup basketball game she had seen on her campus. Four black students were playing basketball and liberally using words that are routinely viewed as racial slurs. Four white students watching the game asked if they could join in. The black students said sure, and soon the eight students were playing together. However, the white students, in an effort to be "cool," also began using the traditionally degrading word. The student told us that within minutes a fight broke out.

The public use of degrading words that have been "taken back" may inadvertently signal to others that such usage is appropriate in any context. This can create a safety risk, as it did for the college students on the basketball court, when someone who does not belong to the targeted group uses the words. Similarly, when girls and young women "take back" sexually degrading words and routinely use them to degrade one another, boys and young men may feel an increased sense of permission to use these words.

I have seen teachers confront this situation by talking to the students who are "taking back a word." The teachers, recognizing that the students are using the word in a different context, express the concern that other students will mistakenly believe that it is acceptable to use those words in other contexts. These teachers frequently make the distinction between a public and a private space. If the students from a traditionally targeted group want to use words that they have "taken back" in the privacy of their own homes, that is their own personal choice. But if they use those words in a public space, those words are inappropriate and raise issues of safety.

Misunderstood Meanings

Often, particularly in elementary and middle school, students use degrading words that they do not understand. Faculty then face a different challenge: determining the best way to explain to a student why a word is degrading. The answer will depend upon the age of the student and the specific word or slur that was used. With older students, teachers can be more explicit and factual about the meaning of a word and why it is offensive. For example, if an older student uses a racial or ethnic slur in a context that causes a teacher to believe the student does not know the meaning of the word, the teacher can first ask the student if he or she knows what the word means. If the student's answer demonstrates a lack of understanding, the teacher can respond in a number of ways:

• Explain that the word is a very degrading and ugly way to refer to blacks, Asians, Latinos, Jews, Muslims, or whoever the targeted group may be.

• Take the opportunity to discuss the impact of the word by, for example, explaining that a particular slur has been intertwined with violence committed against a particular racial or ethnic group.

• Ask the student to look up the definition of the word and report back.

With younger students, teachers may decide that the student is not mature enough to understand the literal definition. In this situation, the teacher can be less specific about what the word means but still be explicit about how offensive and hurtful the word is. For example, if a younger student uses an antigay word or a sexually degrading word about girls, a teacher may decide that the child is too young to understand the sexual context of the word. The teacher can respond effectively in a number of ways:

• *I don't like hearing that word because many people use it to be mean to [girls or to people who are gay or lesbian].*

• *That word makes [girls or people who are gay or lesbian] feel very bad and sad.*

• *That's not a nice word about [girls or people who are gay or lesbian], and I don't want anyone to use it in this school.*

Sometimes a child will respond by asking, "What is a gay person?" or "What is a lesbian?" Again, faculty can respond in ways that are age appropriate:

• *Gays are men who love other men.*

• *Lesbians are women who love other women.*

Slurs Used Out of Context

Students in schools all over the United States use derogatory words—particularly homophobic words—in contexts that do not seemingly relate to the word's original meaning. For example, students from elementary to high school use the word "gay" as a universal word of disapproval. If two 5th grade girls do not like another girl's sweater, they might say, "That sweater is so gay!" Obviously, they are not suggesting that the sweater is homosexual. Rather, they are using the word "gay" to mean that the sweater is "not cool," "not pretty," "not fashionable."

The problem with the use of the word "gay" in this context is twofold. First, if students repeatedly use or hear others use a word referring to homosexuals in a context that implies something is not cool or is bad, they receive an additional underlying message: that being gay or homosexual is itself bad or not cool. Second, for those students who are gay, lesbian, bisexual, or transgender, or who have a brother or sister or parent who is, the word "gay" never loses its second meaning. These students always understand that if an "uncool" sweater is referred to as "gay," then they or their gay family member is also going to be thought of as "uncool" or worse. Faculty members need to intervene for both of these reasons—and because of the additional concern that once degrading language becomes accepted and normalized, that language may escalate to stronger language, to threats, and finally to violence. The following responses are appropriate:

• *Please use a different word to describe something you don't like— such as that's "not cool."*

• *That word is sometimes used as a mean word to describe gay men or lesbians. I don't want anyone to use that word here.*

Words That Faculty Are Unfamiliar With

At times teachers hear students use words that are unfamiliar but that are being said in a mean-spirited way. Teachers have two options: do nothing or ask the student what the word means. The second option—even if the student does not explain the meaning or does not know—effectively sends the message that the teacher heard the comment and is concerned about whether it is appropriate.

Disparaging Faculty "Jokes"

In conversations with teachers and other school staff about intervening when degrading comments are made, someone usually asks how to handle disparaging "jokes" in the faculty room. For many people who belong to or have family members who belong to different racial, ethnic, religious, gender, sexual orientation, or dis-ability groups, degrading jokes are upsetting and disillusioning. Often these jokes make teachers feel excluded from their colleagues, particularly when no one speaks up to say that the joke is inappro-priate.

When no faculty member responds to disparaging jokes, the teacher who feels targeted by the joke (because, for example, he or she has a daughter who is a lesbian or is about to adopt a child from a different racial background) is likely to also feel that everyone in the room thought the joke was funny. This is usually not the case; frequently we are very uncomfortable with degrading jokes but do not know how to react. There is no magic way to respond to demeaning jokes—but for the teachers who feel targeted, any response is greatly appreciated.

Appropriate responses can take the form of verbal statements:

- *I don't find that funny.*
- *I don't appreciate that comment.*
- *Language, please!*
- *Please don't make fun of [name of group] in front of me.*
- *I am offended by that joke.*

Responses can also be nonverbal. For many of us, nonverbal responses are easier to make than verbal ones. Appropriate nonver-bal responses include getting up and walking away, not laughing, and staring at the joke teller and shaking your head.

Finally, it is important to realize that when faculty members make degrading jokes or comments among themselves, students may be affected. Students have acute hearing. The doors to faculty rooms may be left open, and the walls are never as soundproof as we might wish. When students hear faculty make degrading comments and no other faculty member intervenes, the message is clear: disrespect is acceptable. If we want to change a climate of disrespect in our schools, we need to include and, indeed, start with the disrespect shown by our colleagues.

Degrading Language Targeted Toward a Particular Student

When a teacher walking through the halls hears a student direct a slur at a particular student in a tone or with words that are threatening or intimidating, the teacher must recognize that language has now escalated to a more serious level—a level that may involve a bias-motivated threat constituting a crime. It is critical in this situation to interrupt the conversation and to clearly state that the language used is unacceptable. But more is needed. The teacher needs to take the student who made the intimidating comment to the principal's office (or to whoever handles this kind of disciplinary problem). Equally important, the teacher or some other faculty member needs to talk privately with the targeted student to see if he or she is OK. Alternatively, the teacher can remove the targeted student from the situation ("John, please come with me. I'd like to talk with you.") and report the names of the offending students to an administrator. Finally, school administrators will need to address this both as a disciplinary matter and as a possible crime requiring immediate referral to the police.

The Importance of Following Instincts

Intervening to address the lower levels of harassment can create safety in another way. The teachers who most consistently interrupt harassment also develop a sixth sense or instinct as to when conduct is likely to escalate to violence.

Several years ago I interviewed a high school boy in the course of investigating a hate crime. Many of his classmates considered the boy to be gay. He described one particular occasion when several larger boys started taunting him in school with antigay slurs and threats. Without the boys realizing it, an English teacher in the school overheard the comments. The teacher responded immediately by telling the boys that this type of language was absolutely unacceptable in that school. The teacher then asked John whether he was okay, and John said that he was fine.

At the end of the school day John started walking down the long hill from the school into the center of town. The boys who had been taunting him soon began following him, yelling antigay slurs interlaced with threats. John started walking faster, and so did the boys. John started to break into a run, and the boys did the same. At that moment, perhaps seconds before a serious injury or worse might have occurred, the English teacher pulled up in his car next to John. He got out of his car and asked John to get in the car so that he could drive him home. He then faced the other boys, took each of their names, and told them that he would report this incident immediately to the school's principal.

When I spoke to the teacher the next day, I asked him how he had happened to be driving his car down the hill at that moment. He told me it was not a coincidence. After the incident in the hallway, he had been left with a strong sense of disquiet about John's safety. He decided to follow John down the hill to make sure that he was okay. That John, in fact, was okay—that he was not beaten up—was due to the unheralded commitment of one English teacher to follow his instincts.

Learning Necessary Intervention Skills

I find that some faculty members, for a variety of reasons, have difficulty intervening to interrupt degrading language and slurs. Some adults are unaware of the destructive impact of language; others are unsure what is appropriate to say; and others get into the habit, as more than one teacher has told me, of "shutting down" their ears as they walk through the halls. Many teachers, staff, and administrators can use help in addressing these issues and concerns. Intervening is a skill, and, like other skills involved in teaching, it can be taught and practiced (and practiced some more).

Many schools start focusing on this issue by conducting inservice workshops for faculty. Effective workshops explore the pervasiveness of degrading language in the school and the effect of that language on students; they provide an opportunity for faculty to work in groups in thinking through how to respond to real-life scenarios of harassment. Providing faculty the opportunity to practice what works and what does not work is a critical component of any training on preventing harassment and violence.

In working with faculty on effective interventions, administrators should keep in mind the following points:

• Inservice workshops are important *beginnings*, but they must not be the end of the effort. Administrators need to keep this issue before their faculty regularly.

• Administrators need to model consistent interventions for faculty and staff.

• Administrators need to regularly remind teachers and staff at faculty meetings of the importance of speaking up to interrupt harassment.

• Periodically, portions of inservice days can be spent having faculty work on scenarios to practice effective ways to intervene.

• Administrators can track data on the extent of harassment in schools and regularly report the results to faculty. Using school climate data (from surveys, beeper studies, and interviews) as a formative tool for measuring the scope of problems, prioritizing the problems that require the most attention, and then monitoring change or progress in these targeted areas is a powerful strategy for keeping faculty informed on the extent of harassment.

The Effect of Intervention

Interrupting the Pattern of Escalation

Faculty who consistently and firmly interrupt the use of degrading language break the pattern of escalation from the lower levels of verbal harassment, to stronger language, to threats, and, finally, to violence. When the escalation is prevented, schools become safer places.

The Effect on Bystanders

When degrading language is used, many of us tend to judge the impact of our interventions by whether we have succeeded in stopping students from saying the offending word again. But this is only one measure of the effectiveness of intervening. I have spoken to many teachers who become increasingly disheartened that their interventions are ineffective because they hear the students they interrupted continue to use degrading language and slurs. In fact, one of the most powerful impacts of interrupting the use of degrading language may be invisible to most teachers.

Although reducing the use of degrading language is a major concern, an equal concern is the impact of that language on students who feel that the language is targeted at them. The teacher who hears two students use a slur while walking in the hallway and is deciding whether to intervene may not know which other students are walking nearby. One of those students may have an older brother or sister (or a parent) who is gay or a favorite first cousin who is black. That student likely will interpret the degrading language as being targeted at herself or himself or at a beloved family member. Moreover, those students, although accustomed to hearing slurs in the hallway, are likely to be devastated if an adult (particularly an adult whom they admire) walks by and says nothing. Conversely, when teachers intervene, the effect on those students who believe they are the target can be extraordinarily powerful.

Giving Children Back Their Hope

Teachers who routinely interrupt degrading language save some students from having to experience the fear, the anger, and the loss of spirit that all too frequently are the results of harassment. It is striking that students do not forget those teachers who step up to confront bias, prejudice, and harassment. I talk not only to high school students but also to former students in their 20s, 30s, 40s, and beyond about their experiences with harassment in high school. It no longer surprises me to hear from these men and women that they remember with crystal clarity the teacher who spoke up to protect them.

Recently, I was having a telephone conversation with a 57-year-old man who had called to discuss a current civil rights issue. During the course of the conversation, he started talking about his high school experiences. He explained that he was an Arab American who had moved to the United States from the Middle East at age 12. He described an incident that occurred at the end of an algebra class when he was 16 years old. After the bell had rung and students were gathering their books and beginning to leave the classroom, some students started taunting him with anti-Arab slurs. His algebra teacher, who was halfway out the door, immediately turned and walked back into the classroom. She stood directly in front of the boys and with an uncompromising stare said in an equally uncompromising voice that no one in her class would ever speak in a degrading or derogatory fashion toward any student because of who they were, where they were from, or what they believed in. "Not now, and not ever again," she said.

Several minutes after our conversation ended, I realized that this 57-year-old man had described the incident as if it had occurred earlier that day. In fact, it had occurred 41 years ago! All these years later that algebra teacher was still this man's heroine. When this man reaches the age of 67, 77, or 87, he most likely will continue to recall with intensity and warmth that teacher who spoke up for respect.

When teachers intervene to stop harassment, they provide targeted students with an extraordinary and valuable asset: a faith in
the courage of people to stand up for respect and dignity. This faith
can outlast and overcome the despair and degradation that prejudice and harassment all too often leave in their wake.

Role Modeling Civility for Students

Perhaps most important, when teachers, guidance counselors,
nurses, coaches, administrators, and others intervene to interrupt
the use of degrading language, they model the confidence and skills
necessary for students to stand up and speak up for civility and
respect. Faculty cannot change a culture of incivility alone—they
need the help of students. (See Chapter 7 for a discussion of the
importance of peer leader programs that empower students to stand
up and speak up for others who are the targets of harassment.)

5

ADDRESSING THE NEEDS OF VICTIMIZED STUDENTS

David had been in his new high school for only about two weeks when the rumors started that he was gay. Within days after the rumors began, David began hearing slurs directed at him in the hallways, in the cafeteria, in classrooms when teachers were out of the room, and in the bathrooms. Over the next several weeks, more and more students said these slurs to David's face; at the same time the slurs became more and more graphic and hostile. This constant humiliating and degrading language continued throughout the fall; however, at the end of October, the first of the far more serious incidents occurred.

David lived with his mother and brother in an apartment across the street from the school's athletic fields. At the end of the school day, as he stepped into the street on his way to his apartment, David heard a car engine revving at an unusually high pitch. At first, he did not think anything of it. But by the time he was halfway across, the engine noise was much louder, and he turned to see a car bearing down on him at a very fast speed. He started to walk quickly and then finally to run. As he stepped onto the curb, the car brushed his backpack, spinning him around 180 degrees and causing him to fall to the ground. As he looked up, he saw two classmates in the car. The student on the passenger side made eye contact with him and, using an antigay slur, yelled, "Run, David, run!" David got up and did just that; he ran to his second-floor apartment and spent the next hour and a half looking out the window to see if these two boys would return. He was hoping that the boys did not know where he lived. David did not tell any adult within or outside the school about this incident.

The verbal harassment continued every day throughout the rest of the fall. However, in his Spanish class, two other boys engaged in a far more aggressive pattern of harassment toward David. Whenever the teacher stepped out of the room for a minute or turned to write something on the board, these two boys would either whisper jokes about David or would get out of their chairs and tape messages to his desk or to his back. The messages contained degrading antigay comments. Shortly before the Christmas recess, the Spanish class went to the home economics room to prepare a Spanish meal. David was standing next to some other students preparing vegetables. When the teacher stepped out of the room for a minute, David heard his name called. Turning, David saw one of the boys who had been harassing him standing in front of him holding a paring knife less than an inch from David's throat. The boy looked straight at David and asked, "Want me to cut your throat and put you out of your misery?" David described this scene as if it were occurring in slow motion. Time seemed to slow down; no one did or said anything. Then the teacher walked back into the room. Time speeded up and everybody went back to their places and acted as if nothing had happened. Again, David did not tell any adult at the school about this incident.

Early in January after the Christmas break, David was coming out of the boys' bathroom when a much larger and older student bumped into him and told him, using graphic, degrading antigay language, that people like him should not use the boys' bathroom and that instead he should use the girls' bathroom. The student went on to tell David that if he ever found him in the boys' bathroom again, he would seriously beat him. Again, David did not tell any adults about what had happened.

A couple of weeks later David finally told his mother about these incidents. She immediately went to school officials and to law enforcement authorities. At that point, the school reacted aggressively to address the specific incidents; the local police department investigated, and the Attorney General's Office filed a civil rights enforcement action in court.

Approximately a month after the case had ended, I called David's mother to see how he was doing. When I made the call, I believed that the system had reacted extremely well in addressing David's needs. David's mother, however, changed those assumptions. She told me that David was not doing very well and that he would be going into the hospital the next morning for reconstructive surgery on his bowels. It turned out that beginning in October, shortly after the incident when he had almost been run over by a car, David had stopped going to the bathroom in school because he believed the bathroom was not a safe place for him. The problem was compounded because David started getting to school an hour early and leaving one to two hours late in order to avoid walking home when other students were around. David did this to minimize the chance of experiencing another violent incident like the one that occurred when the two classmates tried to run him over. The combination of not going to the bathroom for 10 to 11 hours a day and the anxiety and fear that David experienced created serious intestinal problems that ultimately required surgery. David continues to suffer the effects of those intestinal problems and likely will do so for the rest of his life.

David's story, unfortunately, is not unique. Many students feel a similar reluctance to disclose harassment to adults, leading to two serious consequences. First, as was discussed in Chapter 1 and is illustrated by David's own experiences, verbal harassment can escalate to threats and to violence unless adults within the school confront it. Second, the emotional and physical effects of harassment, if harassment is allowed to continue day after day, week after week, and month after month, can grow in severity. Both of these consequences emphasize the critical importance of administrators, faculty, and staff working to create a climate that maximizes the possibility of early disclosure of harassment.

Students' Reluctance To Disclose Harassment

As discussed in Chapter 3, whether students are victims of harassment or bystanders, they are reluctant to disclose harassment for similar reasons:

• They fear retaliation from students if they report incidents to adults.

• They fear that adults in the school will treat the harassment as if it is only a minor problem.

Data gathered by William Preble and others demonstrate that students become increasingly reluctant to report harassment as they move into higher grades (2002). Many students, both victims and bystanders, are reluctant to report harassment when they do not see a clear and firm commitment on the part of the school to aggressively deal with harassment, threats, and violence.

Maximizing the Possibility of Early Disclosure

Administrators, teachers and other staff, and students can work to create a school climate that provides students who are the victims of harassment with the confidence to disclose that harassment to someone else. Just as important, for students who either learn of harassment directly from a friend or see harassment occurring in the halls, a civil and respectful climate can encourage them to disclose what occurred. It is hard to overestimate the importance of students' providing information to adults about harassment at an early point. Only early intervention can stop the pattern of escalation from words to stronger words, to threats, to violence. Early intervention also can save some students from having to experience the fear, anger, and loss of hope that often result from harassment. It is almost certain that, with early intervention, David would not have had to undergo surgery or experience a life filled with medical problems. With early intervention, students at countless other schools would not have to experience the physical damage and emotional scars of ongoing, terrifying, and humiliating harassment.

• *Superintendents, principals, and other school administrators* have the power to create a school climate that not only treats harassment as a serious problem but also cultivates the innate courage and leadership of students. When administrators immediately respond to harassment, they send a message to students that they will *listen* and *respond* to complaints. Students then will be more willing to report incidents of harassment to teachers and administrators. Administrators should take a number of concrete steps to demonstrate their commitment to creating safe and respectful schools.

Working in tandem with school boards, administrators should create clear and explicit antiharassment policies and then ensure that those policies are effectively enforced. Administrators should also regularly provide messages to faculty, staff, students, and parents about the destructive power of harassment and the importance of everyone in the school community working to create a safe and respectful school climate. Administrators can speak to the entire school, send letters to parents and community members, bring in outside speakers and presenters, and act in countless other ways to become leaders in an effort to create respectful and civil school environments. Just as important, administrators should provide training and workshops to their faculty and staff on how to address harassment. Finally, and most important, administrators should provide support and resources for programs that help students to develop leadership skills, as well as the knowledge and confidence to intervene at the lower levels of harassment before it escalates to more serious misconduct.

• *Teachers and staff* also play a critical role in creating a climate that maximizes the possibility that students will have the confidence to disclose harassment. Perhaps most important, teachers and staff need to model for students techniques of intervening in low-key but firm ways when students use degrading language or slurs. When these incidents occur in classrooms, teachers need to take advantage of the "teachable moment" to discuss the destructive power of degrading language.

• *Students*—particularly those who participate in peer leader programs—can develop the knowledge, confidence, and skills to intervene when verbal harassment occurs and to report to an adult when they believe that harassment has escalated to more serious levels. Ultimately, when students turn from mere bystanders to harassment to active citizens willing to protect others, school climate can change significantly.

Responding to Students Who May Be Victims

There is no one way for teachers, staff, and administrators to assist or respond to students who have been harassed. However, the following general guidelines can be helpful.

Relying on Instincts

Teachers, staff, and administrators develop good instincts about the young people they are working with. It is important to follow those instincts. Look for signs that a student is troubled, such as lower grades, reduced ability to concentrate, increased insecurity, dropping out of extracurricular activities, weight loss or gain, and lack of participation in class. When your instincts tell you that a student is troubled, following up is critical, even if the nature of the trouble is unknown:

• Try to talk to the student directly.

• Refer the student to the guidance counselor, social worker, school nurse, or other person to whom the student might be willing to talk.

• Create trust with students by making yourself available to talk, being honest, and showing you care about their problems.

• If the student describes harassment that appears serious or involves criminal conduct, refer the matter immediately to administrators for possible disciplinary action under antiharassment policies and for possible referral to police.

Talking with Students

Guidance counselors, social workers, school nurses, coaches, teachers, and administrators all find themselves in situations that involve talking with a student whom they believe is troubled. No single interview technique will be 100 percent successful. To talk with a student about any problem, including the possibility of bias-motivated harassment, requires that adults be flexible. They need to use their skills and intuition in finding the best way to enlist the trust and confidence of the young person to whom they are talking. Although it is unlikely that every student will disclose harassment or violence, the interviewer can do several things to maximize the possibility of disclosure.

Naming Possible Problems. Many young people experiencing harassment or violence do not believe that adults in their school will take their problem seriously. Naming potential problems can go a long way to assuring young people both that the interviewer is aware of the kind of problem they are experiencing and that it is safe to talk about it.

Teenagers who seek help frequently report a set of symptoms such as anxiety, depression, sleeplessness, and declining grades, among others. Such symptoms could be caused by bias-motivated harassment or by a range of other social or health-related problems. The interviewer can suggest to the young person that these symptoms could be caused by many factors, including, for example, sexual harassment, bias-motivated harassment, dating violence, sexual abuse, domestic violence, or substance abuse. (The interviewer could say, for example, "I know of girls who are harassed in school because others think that they are lesbians, or are being harassed and even subjected to violence by their boyfriends . . . .") By mentioning the type of problems other students experience, the interviewer assures the student that the problem is understood to be real and substantial. Even if the student does not disclose the problem, the fact that the problem has been named and its importance validated may give the young person the confidence to disclose to someone else.

Avoiding Gender-Specific Language. In talking with a young person, it is critical to avoid using language that assumes that the student is involved in heterosexual relationships. Use of language that suggests that a young person is having dating relationships or sexual relationships with someone of the opposite sex (such as asking a girl if she is dating any boys) is likely to discourage gay, lesbian, bisexual, transgender, or questioning students from disclosing either their sexual orientation or the existence of antigay harassment or violence. Instead, it is important to develop a vocabulary that is gender-neutral. For example, the interviewer may ask a girl whether she is dating "anyone" or whether she is engaged in sexual activity with "anyone." Generally, heterosexual students will not be aware of the language shift, but gay/lesbian/bisexual/transgender/questioning students will clearly interpret this as an important signal: that it is safe to talk about issues of sexual orientation, including antigay harassment.

Avoiding Promises That Can't Be Kept. In the years I directed the Civil Rights Unit within the State Attorney General's Office, one of the few rules I provided to prosecutors was never to make a promise that they could not keep. This rule meant never to promise confidentiality.

Everyone who works with young people—whether as educators, health professionals, or police officers—has one clear, overriding responsibility: to protect the safety of the children with whom they work. Whenever a student discloses something that involves a risk of physical or emotional danger either to that student or to someone else, responsible adults must take the appropriate action to make sure that our young people are safe. Moreover, it is appropriate to take a conservative view of what constitutes a risk to safety, given the escalation that can occur from relatively minor levels of verbal harassment to more serious verbal harassment, to threats, to violence. Given the destructive, and even life-threatening, physical and mental effects of harassment on our young people, acting on information concerning harassment toward students must occur at the earliest moment and in the most appropriate way.

Many people are concerned that young persons will refuse to disclose their problems if their request for confidentiality cannot be honored. Although this happens on occasion, in my experience it happens only rarely. Most students who ask a teacher to keep harassment confidential are really asking for two contradictory things. First, they are asking for secrecy; second, they are asking for help. These students want someone to *stop* the harassment. Teachers can use a number of different approaches to help students become comfortable with reporting harassment to the appropriate person:

• Teachers can ask students what worries them about reporting harassment. Most often students are afraid of retaliation. Teachers can explain that retaliation *usually* does not occur when schools react firmly and quickly, but that harassment will most likely continue and may escalate to something far more serious if nothing is done.

• Teachers can strategize with students about different ways to report harassment to school administrators (or to police if the harassment involves threats or violence).

• Teachers can offer to go with students to report harassment, or teachers can offer to report incidents without students present. Some students may feel more comfortable if a close friend goes with them to meet with the principal or other administrator.

No one approach will work with every student. In rare instances, no approach will succeed in making a student feel comfortable about reporting harassment. In those instances, teachers need to explain that it is their responsibility to make sure that the student is safe and that they need to report the harassment. Teachers must not take the risk of not reporting harassment—the risk that several days later they will pick up the morning newspaper and learn that the boy or girl who had spoken to them about harassment is now in the hospital being treated for a broken bone, a serious concussion, or even worse. Adults' obligation is to report harassment *immediately*—with or without the agreement of the student.

Addressing Parents' Concerns. Sometimes parents will accompany their child to a meeting with a counselor or an administrator. Moreover, some parents request or even demand that they be present during interviews with their child. It is extremely important to conduct interviews with young people who are expressing stress and anxiety outside the presence of parents. It is unlikely that a student will disclose violence or sexual abuse in the home while a parent is present. Similarly, for many gay/lesbian/bisexual/transgender or questioning children, the disclosure of antigay, bias-motivated harassment in front of their parent may "out" the students to their parent and create issues of safety in the home.

One way to address concerns of parents is to provide them an opportunity to discuss their issues or observations at the beginning of the meeting and then to have them wait outside while the student is interviewed. It is also helpful to explain to the parent that it is the school's policy in all instances to have these types of meetings with the student alone.

Reference

Preble, W., Taylor, L., & Langdon, S. (2002). When no one is watching: School climate research from 30 schools. Keynote address, Annual Summer Institute, New England College, Henniker, NH.

6

THE ROLE OF ADMINISTRATORS

Superintendents, principals, and other administrators have a difficult and critical role in creating and maintaining a climate of civility and respect within their schools. Administrators must adopt sound and effective antiharassment policies, develop and consistently administer the disciplinary sanctions contained in those policies, and institute *appropriate* security measures for their schools. At the same time, however, school administrators must give voice to respect and civility in their interactions with faculty and staff, with students, and with the community. In my experience, the principals who are most successful in maintaining a safe and respectful school environment are those who put the appropriate structural components into place but then rely on more traditional and visible components of leadership: becoming a spokesperson for civility and respect.

Creating Structures for Ensuring Safety

Schools need to have key structural components in place to ensure a safe and respectful school climate.

The structural components include antiharassment policies, training for faculty and staff, and—if, and only if, appropriate—security measures.

Effective and Comprehensive Antiharassment Policies

Antiharassment policies are a critical building block of any school's effort to address harassment, bullying, and violence. Several years ago, I participated in a working group charged with writing a guide for schools on addressing harassment. The working group consisted of representatives of the Office of Civil Rights of the United States Department of Education and the National Association of Attorneys General. The guide, entitled *Protecting Students from Harassment and Hate Crime* (1999), provides excellent recommendations on the creation of antiharassment policies. The following section relies, in part, on those recommendations.

Expressing the School's Commitment. The specific provisions contained in an antiharassment policy are critical. However, it is equally important that the policy begin with a broad statement articulating the school's commitment to preventing and responding to harassment. Such a statement sends a critical message to every member of the school community about the importance of creating an educational environment that is both safe and respectful for every student.

Coverage. Antiharassment policies should cover all categories of harassment prohibited by applicable federal and state law and should also include an overarching prohibition of all harassment. Currently, federal education statutes prohibit conduct that creates a hostile educational environment based on race, color, disability, national origin, and sex. Many state laws add additional categories.

In my view, schools should go beyond the categories of harassment or discrimination covered in federal and state law. Antiharassment policies should also include those additional categories of harassment that present significant problems for students.

Survey data collected by William Preble as well as anecdotal data collected by the Center for the Prevention of Hate Violence (CPHV) show that harassment based on *sexual orientation, physical appearance, and socioeconomic status* is widespread in schools (Preble, Taylor, & Langdon, 2002).

Some administrators may be concerned that the specific inclusion of sexual orientation in harassment policies could become a source of controversy. My experience does not confirm those concerns. CPHV has conducted antiharassment programs for students, faculty, and parents in urban, suburban, and rural schools, many of which are located in politically and religiously conservative areas. In all of our programs, CPHV explicitly addresses antigay harassment along with other types of harassment. The center has never been criticized for presenting information on the destructive impact of antigay harassment. Similarly, the administrators in these schools have never been criticized for inviting us to work with their faculty, students, and community.

I believe that CPHV's success in addressing antigay harassment is based on our focus on stopping harassing conduct without challenging the students' rights to their own beliefs. Students have the right to *hold* beliefs that are hostile to students of color, Jewish students, or gay and lesbian students. However, they do *not* have the right to *act* on those beliefs by using degrading language, engaging in other forms of harassment, or resorting to violence. The center's approach focuses parents, teachers, and students on the three core beliefs that underlie our work:

1. Every child has the right to be physically and emotionally safe at school.
2. Children cannot learn and grow to their fullest potential when they fear for their safety.
3. It is possible to create schools and classrooms where a climate of safety and respect enables all children to thrive and succeed.

In my experience, these core beliefs have wide acceptance in communities throughout the United States. Faculty, staff, and parents in urban, rural, and suburban schools have joined together in focusing on the goal of ensuring that *all* our children—girls and boys, white and black, able and disabled, and heterosexual and gay—are physically and emotionally safe in the hallways and the classrooms of their schools.

Clear Definitions. It is important that antiharassment policies clearly define each category of harassment specifically covered by the policy and provide examples. Without both clear definitions and examples, faculty, staff, administrators, and students may misunderstand harassment policies. If such policies are to be effective, everyone within the school community must understand in very clear and practical terms what constitutes harassment and what the policies prohibit. When members of the school community—particularly faculty and administrators—do not understand what constitutes harassment under each category covered, the result may be an inconsistent and ineffective application of the policy. Additionally, policies that fail to contain clear and precise definitions are more likely to be subject to legal challenges. Administrators should ask their school districts' legal counsel to review antiharassment policies.

Reporting Procedures. Faculty, administrators, staff, and students all need to know how, and to whom, they should report harassment. If information on harassment is not reported to the appropriate school officials, then schools will not be in the position to adequately respond. Antiharassment policies also need to provide educators with clear guidance on the exact circumstances that obligate them to report instances of harassment.

Prohibition of Retaliation. Students frequently report that they are uncomfortable reporting harassment because of fear of retaliation by the perpetrators. Antiharassment policies need to clearly prohibit and establish serious consequences for retaliation against the targets of harassment, as well as toward those students who provide information about harassment directed at some other student. If students are not confident that they will be protected from retaliation, they will be less likely to provide administrators, faculty, and staff with information about harassment that has occurred. The most comprehensive and effective harassment policy will ultimately be ineffective if students do not feel safe in making reports.

Disciplinary Sanctions. Students need to understand the range of disciplinary sanctions that can be imposed for engaging in different types of harassment and other misconduct. A well-constructed antiharassment policy can serve as a deterrent toward harassment—but only if the consequences of student misconduct are clearly set forth.

Informing the School Community of Antiharassment Policies

No antiharassment policy will be fully effective if students, faculty, staff, and administrators are not aware of the policy and do not understand its major components. Consequently, administrators *must* provide each member of the school community with a copy of the written policy. However, school administrators need to go further. School antiharassment policies are formal documents that are often difficult to understand. A knowledgeable person should orally explain the policy and answer questions from students, faculty, and staff several times per year.

Still more is needed, however, if administrators are to ensure that students understand such vitally important policies. Policies should be summarized in clear and straightforward language; these summaries should not only be provided to students but also placed in appropriate places within the school. The creation of colorful, interesting, and readable posters displayed in the school may be the most effective way to keep the provisions of antiharassment policies before students and faculty.

Inservice Training for Faculty, Staff, and Administrators

Antiharassment policies are not self-enforcing. Their effectiveness depends on faculty, staff, and administrators understanding the policies; understanding the importance of consistent enforcement; understanding how and to whom to report harassment; understanding how to handle requests for confidentiality by students reporting harassment; and other related issues. This information can be provided to faculty and staff relatively quickly both in meetings before the school year begins and at faculty/staff meetings. It is particularly important that all new faculty and staff receive this information as soon as possible after they begin work at a school.

The core of inservice training aimed at preventing harassment, however, does not lie in the explanation of antiharassment policies. Rather, school administrators need to provide mandatory, periodic, and interactive workshops that provide participants with an understanding of the impact of harassment, both in terms of its tendency to escalate to more serious misconduct and, even in the absence of escalation, its devastating emotional impact on students who are targeted. Most important, inservice trainings on preventing harassment must provide faculty and staff with practical skills for intervening immediately when students use degrading language or slurs. Intervention to interrupt the use of degrading language and slurs (described in Chapter 4) comes naturally to some faculty and staff but is more difficult for others. Inservice training is a key component in giving teachers the confidence and skills to speak up in consistent and low-key ways when students reflexively and without any intent to harm use degrading language and slurs.

Security Measures

Since the highly publicized multivictim school shootings in Littleton, Colorado, San Diego, California, and elsewhere, school administrators nationally have effected a variety of security measures including metal detectors at the front doors of the school, video cameras on buses and in halls, more police officers within the school, and mock school shooting exercises involving the entire school community. School administrators must take an objective and calm look at the security needs of their schools. Not every school needs enhanced security. Trained school resource officers who interact with students in a variety of friendly and helpful ways can greatly assist in creating a respectful school climate and in determining what, if any, additional security measures are appropriate for the school.

Unfortunately, the recent multivictim shootings have brought about a reflexive overreaction by some school administrators. Security measures have been implemented without a realistic assessment of whether those measures are necessary. Adverse consequences may result from the introduction and use of unneeded security measures. Such measures—the use of video cameras on every school bus and in the corridors, the use of metal detectors at school entrances and exits, and the routine search of student lockers—send a clear and disturbing message to students. If our solution to school violence is surveillance of every student, metal detection applied to every student, random searches of lockers of every student, then the signal we give is that *every student* is the problem. We know that the problem of school violence is complex; moreover, we all know that the vast majority of students want a respectful and safe school environment. Many students are natural leaders. With support and training they can become powerful agents to help create safe schools. Instead, they can easily become disillusioned, disheartened, and disempowered by the constant messages that the source of the problem of school harassment and violence is every student. We can do better. Our students deserve it.

Recently, some schools have begun using mock disasters—specifically, mock school shootings—as a means of training the entire community on how to react to such terrible situations. This approach to keeping our schools safe raises three concerns. First, school shootings in the United States are *rare* (Centers for Disease Control and Prevention, 2001). In fact, during the 1990s, the number of school shootings declined (U.S. Department of Health and Human Services, 2000). Training students on how to respond to situations that are extraordinarily unlikely to occur in any given school is a questionable use of valuable resources. Second, tragedies rarely occur as planned or expected. The scenario that schools choose for their mock demonstration may bear little resemblance to the tragedy that actually occurs. Accordingly, the guidance that students receive on what to do, where to go, and how to act may not be the appropriate or even safe guidance for an actual occurrence. Finally, the use of mock demonstrations of school shootings scares students. Recently I conducted an orientation program for the entire first-year class at a college. At the close of the event, students had the opportunity to talk about issues that had arisen in their high school. Student after student—each from different high schools— stood up to express how fearful they had become of multivictim shootings as a result of the mock scenarios of tragedies that they were required to participate in. The security measures being enacted by many schools to keep students safe may have the unintended effect of making them more anxious and scared.

Giving Voice to Respect

There is no more critical leadership skill than articulating—and then rearticulating again and again—the importance of creating a civil and respectful educational climate. Well-structured and comprehensive antiharassment policies, comprehensive faculty training, and appropriate security measures will not create a safe and respectful school atmosphere unless the leaders within the school and the school system model the importance of maintaining a respectful, civil school environment.

Superintendents

Although the responsibility for developing and maintaining a safe school lies primarily with the building principal, school superintendents also play a critical role. Superintendents should speak to faculty either at districtwide meetings or faculty meetings about the importance of creating a safe, respectful climate for every student. Similarly, superintendents should constantly reiterate this message in meetings with their school board and with parents and community groups. Most important, superintendents should set the tone and the example for their principals and other senior administrators. Both in regular meetings, workshops, and one-on-one communications with principals and other administrators, superintendents need to give voice to the importance of maintaining respectful environments.

Principals

The role of principals in expressing the importance of creating a safe, respectful school begins on the first day that faculty arrive at the end of the summer and ends on the last day of school. Principals should stress the importance of preventing harassment in many ways: speaking at regularly scheduled faculty meetings, convening schoolwide assemblies, and visiting each class for several minutes. Similarly, those principals who communicate to parents in letters (either sent home with students or mailed) and in meetings for parents and the community are most effective in enlisting broader support for creating a safe, respectful school climate. Finally, principals need to raise the importance of addressing bias, harassment, and violence both in meetings with senior districtwide administrators and with their school board.

Faculty and staff and students cannot be expected to develop the confidence and skills for intervening to stop the routine use of degrading language unless they see their administrators role modeling those same skills. Administrators have a responsibility to speak up to interrupt the use of degrading language whether it occurs among students in the hallway, teachers in the faculty lounge, or senior administrators at a districtwide meeting.

Many of us know at least one principal who came into a school filled with problems of bias, harassment, disrespect, and even violence. Slowly, by the force of her voice, the resources she fought for, and the power of her modeling, she changed the lives of teachers, students—indeed, the entire climate of the school. Not every one of us is the same type of leader. Not every one of us is a powerful public speaker. Not every one of us is a passionate communicator one-on-one. And not every one of us has the same ability to advocate effectively in a highly charged school board meeting. But each of us has our own leadership style; each of us is able to give voice in our own way to the importance of civility. We all are able to advocate for needed resources and to model the behavior that we want our students, faculty, parents, and community to both appreciate and incorporate into their own lives. The process of changing school climate cannot be accomplished by principals, superintendents, and other administrators alone. However, the creation of safe, respectful learning environments is extraordinarily difficult without *committed* and *visible* leadership.

Responding to School Violence

Schools may take all the appropriate measures to prevent harassment from escalating to a serious incident of threat or violence, and yet such incidents can still occur. The response taken by school administrators, faculty, and staff toward serious incidents of harassment, violence, and even hate crimes can significantly affect the future climate at the school, the impact of the incident on the victim and others, and the risk of retaliation.

Appropriate Reporting

Threats and violence obviously cannot be addressed unless they are reported to school administrators. Although faculty and staff obviously do not report every incident of incivility committed by students, it is critically important to report every serious incident of harassment, every threat of violence, and every act of violence. Faculty and staff must report these incidents *immediately* to the appropriate administrator.

Similarly, not every incident involving serious harassment involves criminal conduct. However, when harassment rises to the level of threats or violence, school administrators need to make prompt reports to local police. The most effective way for school officials to ensure that local police will react appropriately, promptly, and sensitively to incidents that occur in a school is for school administrators and police to work as partners. Effective partnerships need to be established *before* an incident occurs.

Responding to Graffiti

Graffiti that is threatening to a particular individual or to a group (such as racist, homophobic, or anti-Semitic graffiti) presents a constant message of anger and violence. I have dealt with too many situations in which school administrators have left degrading and bias-motivated graffiti on school walls for days, weeks, and sometimes even months. In one instance, a teacher was concerned that racist graffiti painted on the outside wall of the school gym had been on the building for several weeks. When she asked the principal why it had not been removed, he explained that the custodial department had said that it was not possible to paint over the graffiti in the middle of the winter. Twenty-five minutes later, after I had telephoned the principal to explain the destructive impact of racist graffiti, the custodial staff had found a way to eradicate the graffiti.

However, it is possible to move too quickly to remove graffiti. I have had the unenviable task of trying to prosecute cases of bias-motivated graffiti when no photograph had been taken of the graffiti. It is extremely hard to provide a judge or jury with a sense of the impact of graffiti when they have no photograph to examine. Accordingly, principals and other administrators should immediately seek advice from police when bias-motivated graffiti appears on a building. If police are not going to be able to get to the school in a reasonable amount of time, the graffiti can either be covered up with paper or photographed (with the consent of the police) and then removed.

Addressing the Perpetrators

School administrators need to apply their antiharassment policies by taking appropriate disciplinary measures against students who have perpetrated serious harassment, threats, or violence. Similarly, administrators need to respond quickly and firmly to any retaliation directed toward either the victims of harassment or violence or to witnesses who have made complaints to school administrators.

Administrators must enforce antiharassment policies with consistency. Both William Preble's survey data and anecdotes from students participating in CPHV programs reveal that many students believe teachers and administrators apply antiharassment policies far more aggressively for known bullies than they do toward honor students, athletes, and students with positive relationships with adults in the school (Preble, Taylor, & Langdon, 2002). Inconsistent application of policies can easily lead to distrust in faculty and administrators, increased cynicism, and decreased willingness to follow school rules.

Addressing the Emotional Impact on Students

School administrators need to focus immediately on providing the targets of harassment and bias with counseling and, when appropriate, medical care. Just as important, the principal should meet with the targeted students and their parents to discuss the incident and to express how sorry she or he is about what has occurred. I have seen too many students and their parents become increasingly disillusioned and angry with the school because the principal has not taken the time to express concern and to explain what the school is doing to address the issue. A critical part of the healing process for victims and their families is personal contact with the principal.

The impact of serious harassment, threats, or violence goes beyond the immediate target of the misconduct. Students who belong to the same group as the targeted student (racial, religious, ethnic, sexual orientation, and so on) may be adversely affected emotionally by the incident. Similarly, students who do not belong to the same group but who have personally experienced harassment may also feel scared and anxious as a result of an incident directed at another student, even a student they do not know. Part of the healing process for these students, as well as for the entire school community, is an explanation of what has occurred (without disclosing confidential information) and a strong expression that bias-motivated harassment, threats, and violence are unacceptable within the school community. Principals may address these issues through schoolwide assemblies, visits to every class for brief presentations, and letters addressed to the entire school community.

Faculty and staff must be prepared to respond supportively to the emotional needs of the victims of harassment as well as to the needs of other students who are affected by a serious incident. Frequently I have presented inservice workshops to faculty in the wake of a serious incident of harassment or violence only to find that faculty have no clear idea of what has happened. Principals should communicate to faculty shortly after a serious incident the details of what has occurred and the need to support all students. Principals can provide this type of information—consistent with any concerns for confidentiality—in brief meetings or by using memos or e-mail.

The Risk of Liability

The core reason why administrators need to demonstrate strong leadership focused on preventing and responding to harassment and violence is to create a climate that ensures that every student is safe. However, this kind of leadership also reduces the risk of legal liability for schools. Students and their parents, as well as governmental agencies, have brought suit against schools that they believe have failed to act to protect students from harassment and violence. Although no school is absolutely protected from being sued, the risk of litigation being filed—and certainly the risk of being held liable by a judge or jury—is minimized when administrators demonstrate strong, comprehensive, and vocal leadership focused on preventing and responding to bias, harassment, and violence.

Seizing the Opportunity

Every serious incident of harassment, threat, or violence should be viewed as an opportunity to re-examine the school's efforts to create a respectful environment and to prevent harassment and violence. The fact that a serious incident occurred does not mean that the school has failed. However, any institution needs to periodically re-examine its prevention efforts, and there is no better time to do so than after a serious incident has occurred.

References

Centers for Disease Control and Prevention. (2001). *School health guidelines to prevent unintentional injuries and violence.* Available: http://www.cdc.gov/mmwr/preview/mmwrhtml/rr5022a1.htm.

Preble, W., Taylor, L., & Langdon, S. (2002). When no one is watching: School climate research from 30 schools. Keynote address, Annual Summer Institute, New England College, Henniker, NH.

U.S. Department of Education, Office for Civil Rights and the National Association of Attorneys General. (1999). *Protecting students from harassment and hate crime: A guide for schools.* Washington, DC: Authors. Available: www.ed.gov/pubs/Harassment.

U.S. Department of Health and Human Services. (2000). *Youth violence: A report of the Surgeon General,* Ch. 2. Available: www.surgeon-general.gov/library/youthviolence/.

7

DEVELOPING PEER LEADERS

Recently I conducted an evening program addressing bias, prejudice, and harassment for a group of high school students from schools all over the state of Maine. The students were attending a three-day conference on leadership. At the end of our program, I asked the participating students to talk about incidents in which the intervention of students had made a difference. A young man raised his hand hesitantly. When I called on him, he stood up and began to relate his story. Only two or three days earlier, he had been leaving school at the end of the day when he saw a girl, whose name he did not know, leaving school to get on her bus. He said that the girl looked as if she had the weight of the world on her shoulders. She looked absolutely miserable.

He went on to say that this girl was harassed constantly by a large number of students. When she got on the bus in the morning, she sat by herself. If she decided to sit next to someone, that person invariably moved to another seat. When she arrived at school, students told jokes about her, whispered about her, and made degrading comments directly to her face. He said that only recently he had seen her go into the lunchroom and sit down at a table with four other students. Immediately they moved their trays to another table, laughing at the girl.

The boy said that he looked at the girl as she was about to leave the school to walk to her bus and said, "I hope you have a good afternoon." The girl just stared at him. He was somewhat disconcerted by her response and went on to say, "I hope you are okay. And I really hope you have a good afternoon." He then went to an after-school activity and did not think any more about the encounter.

The next day this boy was the first person home in his family at the end of the day. As he walked through the door and set his books down, he noticed that the light was blinking on the telephone answering machine. He pushed the play button and immediately heard the voice of the girl he had spoken to the prior afternoon. She said his name and then in a soft voice explained that the prior afternoon she had been planning to take the bus home, go up to her mother's bedroom, open the bedside table, and pull out her mother's bottle of antidepressant medication. She said she had been planning to swallow the whole bottle and take her life. The boy said that there was a long pause, and then he heard her say simply, "Thank you." As he sat down the boy said that he still did not know the girl's name. The auditorium full of students remained silent for several minutes.

The power of student leaders to effect change is incalculable. But such change requires empathy and courage. Students all over the United States are making their schools safer, changing lives, and even saving the lives of fellow students. Much of the harassment that goes on within and outside of schools occurs beyond the sight and hearing of adults. If we are going to be successful in creating and maintaining safe and respectful climates in our schools, then we must rely on our single strongest resource—our young people. We must provide our students with the encouragement and skills to move from being bystanders to acting as role models of civility and respect.

Many different models exist for empowering students to take responsibility to stand up and speak up for others. No one model is the right model for every school. One source, "Peer Leadership: Helping Youth Become Change Agents in Their Schools and Communities" (Tiven, 2002), is a publication of Partners Against Hate, a consortium of three civil rights organizations (www.partners-againsthate.org). It provides information on 20 peer leader programs from around the United States. In this chapter, I describe two models that I have developed with colleagues and that have been implemented in Maine and elsewhere.

Peer Leadership Programs

The Maine Attorney General's Civil Rights Team Project

In 1992 my colleague Betsy Sweet and I developed the Civil Rights Team Project at the Office of the Maine Attorney General. The concept was simple: to institutionalize the commitment to addressing bias-motivated harassment and violence by creating teams of student leaders supported by faculty and by the Office of the Attorney General. Each team consists of three or four students per grade and one or two faculty advisors. Most teams met weekly to develop projects that would help focus the attention of the school on addressing bias, prejudice, and harassment. Additionally, the teams and their individual members were available to hear reports of bias-motivated harassment, threats, and violence from students who felt uncomfortable talking to an adult. The responsibility of the teams, upon hearing such complaints, was to pass the information immediately to the appropriate teacher or administrator.

The project started in 1996 with 18 schools in Maine. Seven years later more than 200 schools in Maine have Civil Rights Teams. The teams are located primarily in high schools and middle schools. A number of elementary schools have pilot projects. The members of Civil Rights Teams tend to be socially conscious young people who have shown leadership skills in a variety of proactive ways in their schools. Civil Rights Teams have been involved in an array of projects:

- One team successfully spearheaded an effort to change the name of the school's mascot from one that many Native Americans consider demeaning.

- Many teams have sponsored diversity conferences at their schools.

- One team developed radio public service announcements on combating prejudice.

- One team developed a film series at the school focusing on civil rights.

- Many teams developed procedures through which students could raise issues about harassment.

- Many teams brought speakers to their schools to talk about civil rights issues.

- A number of teams developed, administered, and published schoolwide surveys on the extent of harassment.

- One team spent its spring vacation working with a local artist to produce and place within the school a sculpture focusing on the impact of hate.

- Several teams have made presentations to their school boards and their faculty on the need to address harassment.

During the past seven years the Civil Rights Team Project has raised the level of concern in Maine schools about the problems of bias, harassment, and hate crimes. But the project has done far more. It has provided training and support to several thousand young people who have become self-confident and vocal leaders dedicated to the creation of safe and respectful schools. It has created schools that in the opinion of both students and teachers are safer now than they were several years ago. It has created mechanisms so that students who are reluctant to report incidents to adults can provide that information to peers.

And students do report incidents to their school Civil Rights Teams. In the first year of the project, a student stopped two members of her high school's team in the hall between class periods. She told the team members that as she was leaving her last class a student had yelled an anti-Semitic slur at a Jewish student. The girl said she did not know either of the students very well but she was upset about the incident. The two team members thanked her and immediately went to find one of the team's faculty advisors. That teacher was about to start class but waited while they explained what had just happened. The teacher asked his class to talk quietly for five minutes while he went to the principal's office. The two students then had a short meeting with the principal. Ten minutes after the anti-Semitic slur was made, the offending student was in the principal's office discussing the incident. A response that fast—in any institution, including a school—is remarkable. The principal told us that the actions of the Civil Rights Team had allowed him to intervene *before* the verbal harassment escalated to further harassment or violence.

But the Civil Rights Team Project has done something else. It has provided those students who not only care about issues of civility and respect but also have the confidence and courage to act on those concerns with the knowledge that they are not alone. A memorable example of this effect took place at the closing of the annual statewide Civil Rights Team conference during the first years of the project. A group of students stood on a stage in front of more than a thousand Civil Rights Team members and talked about what the conference had meant for them. One young man gazed with wonder at the hundreds upon hundreds of students in front of him. He said that the most meaningful part of the day was the realization that he was not alone in his commitment and that he was supported not only by the members of his own high school team but by students at middle schools and high schools from every corner of the state.

The CPHV Student Leader Project

In the fall of 1999, shortly after the creation of CPHV, we developed a different model for a peer leader program. Through the Student Leader Project, CPHV works with 40 students from each participating middle school or high school during a full-day workshop, held away from the school facility (Blezard, 2003). The workshop provides students with an understanding of the destructive impact of verbal harassment; it focuses both on the escalation from verbal harassment to more serious violence and on the devastating emotional impact that targeted students experience even without that escalation. The workshop provides students with practical skills for intervening in low-key ways in the hallways, in locker rooms, or on the bus to interrupt students who use degrading language, put-downs, or slurs. The Student Leader Project does not create a new school organization that meets regularly. Instead, it empowers students to act as informal leaders who speak up for civility.

A key component of the Student Leader Project is the broad definition of what it means to be a student leader. CPHV asks each school to select students who are role models and who come from a widely representative set of groups within the school. Most important, CPHV asks schools to include those students who engage in harassment but who are also considered to be leaders and role models by their peers.

CPHV has expanded the program with grant support to reach small and rural schools that do not have the financial resources to bring in programs such as the Student Leader Project. CPHV has worked intensively with very small schools with grade sizes as low as 10 students and as high as 50.

Anecdotes and observations from students, teachers, and administrators indicate the profound impact of the Student Leader Project even on those students generally viewed as "negative" leaders.

One of CPHV's early workshops included a high school junior, a young woman, who argued with us on every point. She did not understand why she was included in the workshop; she disagreed with many of our premises. In fact, at lunchtime she told me that if she wanted to use antigay slurs to refer to other students, that was her right, and if other students objected, it was their problem. Shortly thereafter the principal, who also attended the workshop, told me that he had heeded my request to bring negative leaders to the workshop. This girl, he said, was not only a leader in the school, but was *the* harassment problem in the school!

At the close of each workshop, all 40 students, their faculty advisors, and members of the CPHV staff sit in a circle. We pass around a ball of twine and ask each student to hold on to the twine as the ball is unwound. We explain that the process of speaking up and challenging harassment is far easier when you realize that others will support you. We point out that each student is connected not only by the twine that they are holding, but also by their common experience in spending the day together focusing on addressing bias, prejudice, and harassment. We then pass around a bowl of beads, asking each student to take one bead and state one different thing that they will be able to do the next day in school as a result of the workshop. Many students talk about having the confidence to speak up and interrupt when others use slurs and put-downs. Other students have the courage to admit to their classmates and teachers that they have used slurs in the past and that they will try to speak in different ways. At the end of the exercise, a center staff member cuts the twine to any length requested by the students, who then use the twine and the bead to make necklaces, wrist bracelets, or ankle bracelets. I've seen students still wearing those bracelets weeks and sometimes months after a workshop—reminding themselves of their commitment to be leaders.

Two-thirds of the way around the circle, this particular girl was the next student to speak. I feared that the energy and positive feeling that had been generated by the day's events were about to come crashing down. But she picked up her bead, slowly looked around the entire room, and then said, "Tomorrow when I get to school I am going to go find the kids that I have been harassing and apologize to each of them." A long silence followed her statement.

Shortly after the end of the school year, I spoke with the principal about this incident. This same young woman, he said, had enjoyed a remarkable year. The semester following our workshop was the first semester in her entire middle and high school career in which she had passed every class. It was also the first semester in four years in which she had been suspended only one time. The principal felt this was a result of the workshop. Her participation in the Student Leader Project was the first time that she had ever been asked to be a leader and to take responsibility for something good and positive.

I have heard many similar stories from principals, teachers, and students. Often those students with reputations for harassing and causing trouble are very strong leaders and role models. Unfortunately, they lead in negative ways. I have seen those students, given a chance to exercise their innate empathy, accept the challenge to use their leadership skills in positive ways.

Recently we returned to the first school that participated in the Student Leader Project. This is an extremely diverse high school in which students speak more than 40 different languages in their homes. Present at the meeting were four 9th graders and three 11th graders. The 11th graders had attended our first Student Leader workshop two years earlier; the 9th graders had attended a workshop only six months earlier. All 7 students had been picked randomly from the 160 students who had attended our four Student Leader workshops at the high school over a three-year period. The three 11th graders vividly recalled their work with their classmates during that full-day training. They talked about remaining energized (even two and a half years later) to challenge students in low-key and respectful ways when they used degrading language or put-downs. They also talked about the impact of the project on life at their school. Those three girls commented that students only rarely used degrading language around them and that they believed that there was less harassment in the school.

The four 9th grade students talked about what they had done over the past several months. Two of them, one boy and one girl, discussed how much courage it took to speak up when an older, larger, upper-class student used a put-down or slur. All four 9th graders said that not only were their friends using degrading language less frequently, but some of their friends, who had not attended the workshop, had started to use techniques for interrupting others who use degrading language. At the close of the meeting, a school social worker said that she had seen a dramatic decrease in the number of fights based on race or ethnicity during the past three years.

The Effects of Successful Peer Leader Programs

Not every school peer leader program is equally effective in reducing bias and harassment. With colleagues, William Preble (2002) has surveyed more than 3,000 students, conducted in-depth interviews with more than 300 students, and collected through beeper studies more than 800 documented observations of daily life in classrooms, hallways, and lunchrooms. His evaluations in more than 20 schools show that the effectiveness of peer leader programs in changing school climate varies significantly.

Preble found important indicators of a safe and respectful climate in those schools with the most effective peer leader programs. First, a majority of the students in these schools were aware of the peer leader programs. Second, students from traditionally targeted groups and non-college-bound students reported significantly greater confidence that students and adults would speak up to stop harassment. Third, students perceived a high level of respect from teachers, staff, and administrators. Fourth, all students reported lower levels of harassment and greater feelings of safety.

One additional positive effect was present in *all* schools with peer leader programs. The individual students participating in the programs felt a passion, a pride, and an excitement in working to make their schools safer. Participation in peer leader programs— even those programs that were perceived as less successful—had an overwhelmingly positive effect on those students who were participants. The experience of being a peer leader is empowering.

Preble had an opportunity to interview a number of students who had participated in peer leader programs while they were in middle and high school a few years after they had graduated. When asked which aspects of their involvement in peer leader programs were most effective or memorable, many of these former student leaders told him the same thing. They said that the most powerful part of the whole student leadership experience was "being picked" by adults in their schools as a leader. It had never occurred to most of these students—most of whom had never been elected to a leadership position or run for any student government office—that they could be leaders. They went on to do remarkable things to improve their schools.

Attributes of Effective Peer Leader Programs

Effective antiharassment peer leader programs all build on the same foundation: the innate creativity and leadership abilities of young people. Many students have the capacity for leadership, idealism, and creativity. Many young people not only think "outside of the box" but also do not even know that the box exists. The most effective peer leader programs tap into these traits and empower young people to challenge biases and prejudices and to stick their necks out to make their schools safer and more respectful places.

Preble and colleagues found that effective peer leader programs had most or all of the following characteristics (Preble, Taylor, & Langdon, 2002; van Linden & Fertman, 1998):

• Adults in the school believe in the leadership abilities within all students. They view students as resources for improving schools.

• Participation in the peer leader programs is broad-based, involving many different kinds of students (including those who are academically and nonacademically successful; from diverse social, economic, racial, gender, and sexual orientation groups; popular and less popular).

• Programs have clearly defined missions or goals to guide their work and training.

• The quality of the training for the student leaders is high. This training creates a heightened awareness of the effects of harassment and provides students with concrete skills for changing their school climate.

• The support for peer leaders by their faculty advisors and by administrators is passionate and ongoing but not overbearing. Adults respect the decisions made by student leaders.

• The work of peer leaders is very visible. In these schools a visitor notices the work and commitment of the peer leaders immediately—in the hallways, through posters, bulletin boards, and artwork.

• The most effective programs have been in existence for two or more years, and new members are brought into the program each year.

But no peer leader program exists in a vacuum. Even programs that have displayed most or all of these attributes will not be successful in changing school climate without a broader school commitment to preventing bias, prejudice, and harassment. Student leaders cannot reduce harassment and disrespect by themselves.

Attributes of Safe Schools

The most effective peer leader programs exist within schools that possess multiple points of leadership focusing on respect and civility. Safe and respectful schools begin with *principals and other administrators* who demonstrate visible and committed (and even passionate) leadership. These principals talk with students in the halls, in the cafeteria, and outside of school; intervene in respectful ways when they hear students use degrading language; support and encourage teachers and staff to focus on school climate; and find the resources for faculty training and student programs.

Safe and respectful schools have *faculty* who intervene in the hallways, incorporate materials on diversity and civility into their teaching, and listen to and talk with students. Preble's survey and interview data show that the students in the safest schools perceive that teachers have a high level of respect for students. Teachers show this respect through the interpersonal relations they are willing to develop with students, through the ways they use their knowledge of individual students' strengths and needs to adjust their teaching practices in the classroom, and by the ways they empower students as learners every day through their teaching.

Safe and respectful schools have comprehensive harassment policies that are communicated effectively to faculty, staff, students, and parents. These schools back up their policies with consistent disciplinary actions.

Safe and respectful schools have a variety of *student programs* focusing on different aspects of civility. It is unrealistic to expect that a peer leader program with 10, 20, or even 40 students can by itself change school climate. But when a peer leader program exists side-by-side with other programs, such as diversity clubs, peer mediation programs, key clubs, mentoring programs, gay-straight alliances, and many more, the cumulative effect on school climate can be immense.

There are schools in which students perceive that adults in the school respect them, that adults and students will intervene to stop harassment, and that school is a safe place. Preble's research confirms that these schools pursue a broad range of strategies (including antiharassment peer leader programs) to empower and support students, teachers, and staff in the difficult work of creating safe and respectful environments.

Teachers, staff, and administrators cannot create safe and respectful schools without the help of students. We need to invest the time and resources to develop the empathy and skills of young people to work with adults toward the goal of ending harassment.

References

Blezard, R. (2003, Spring). "We don't use that language anymore": A leadership program helps Maine students confront the culture of verbal abuse. *Teaching Tolerance Magazine, 23,* 32–33.

Preble, W., Taylor, L., & Langdon, S. (2002). When no one is watching: School climate research from 30 schools. Keynote address, Annual Summer Institute, New England College, Henniker, NH.

Tiven, L. (2002). Peer leadership: Helping youth become change agents in their schools and communities. Washington, DC: Partners Against Hate. Available: www.partnersagainsthate.org.

Van Linden, J., & Fertman, C. (1998). *Youth leadership: A guide to understanding leadership development in adolescence.* San Francisco: Jossey-Bass Publishers.

8

RESPONDING TO TERRORISM AND RELATED PREJUDICE

The tragedy of September 11, 2001, spawned two inter-related and lingering problems for children in the United States. First, students in elementary, middle, and high schools across the nation reacted with varying degrees of emotional trauma in the hours, days, weeks, and months after the awful carnage in New York City, Washington, D.C., and rural Pennsylvania. Second, Muslim students, as well as other students mistakenly targeted as Muslim, became the victims of dramatically increased bias, harassment, and violence. We need to understand these problems because the effects are still with us, because terrorist acts remain a national concern, and because we must prevent the continuing prejudice and harassment toward Muslim students.

Terrorism's Impact on Children

The victims of the attacks on September 11 included Christians, Muslims, Jews, Hindus, Americans,

This chapter was cowritten by Bruno Anthony, Associate Professor of Child Psychology at the University of Maryland School of Medicine and Director of the Maryland Center for Attention and Developmental Disorders.

Europeans, Middle Easterners, Asians, Africans, and South Americans. Children in schools throughout the United States—whatever their religion, ethnicity, or nationality—were affected profoundly. In a RAND Corporation national survey in the days following the attacks, more than one-third of children 5 and older disclosed stress symptoms, and almost half said they worried about their safety or that of their families (Schuster et al., 2001).

Children's exposure to violence, either as victims or witnesses, affects their physical health, psychological adjustment, social relations, and academic achievement. Perhaps more disturbing, it affects their views of the world and their ideas about the meaning and purpose of life (Margolin & Gordis, 2000).

Behavioral and Emotional Consequences

Although the types of violence that children experience vary widely, the emotional and behavioral effects of violence have been found to be remarkably similar. The emotional effect on children of high-profile attacks like those of September 11, Oklahoma City, and Columbine High School differs little from the effects of far less publicized community violence in lower-income urban neighborhoods. Children who witness violence in person, on television, or by word of mouth experience a decreased sense of safety and a decreased confidence in the ability of adults to protect them.

Children's immediate reactions to witnessing violence include helplessness, fear, anger, and high arousal (Cicchetti & Toth, 1997). Some children experience severe symptoms of post-traumatic stress disorder, such as intrusive imagery, frightening dreams, emotional constriction and avoidance, fears of recurrence, difficulty falling asleep, increased irritability, and difficulty concentrating.

A child's reactions to trauma may appear immediately after the traumatic event or days or even weeks later and can last for an extended period of time, as the following anecdote illustrates:

Alan's parents had separated in the summer of 2001, and his mother had moved to upstate New York. Alan, age 5, stayed with his father in Baltimore. He was very disturbed by the events of September 11, worrying about his mother's well-being, even though she lived far from New York City. Over the course of the following year, Alan visited his mother several times. Ten months after September 11, Dr. Bruno Anthony talked to him as he built towers made of Lego blocks. He asked several times, "Will New York be killed?" He voiced intense fears about his mother and the danger that might threaten her safety. He intently listened to Dr. Anthony's reassurances, but, on leaving, he asked that his towers not be disturbed until he returned.

The consequences of violence, whether experienced as a victim or a witness, vary in intensity and form depending on the developmental stage of the child (Marans & Adelman, 1997).

Children 5 and Below. Exposure to violence and terror affects children younger than 5, even though they may not fully comprehend the violent episodes. Typical reactions can include a fear of being separated from parents, crying, whimpering, immobility and/or aimless motion, frightened facial expressions, and excessive clinging. Preschoolers living with violence often temporarily lose skills they have previously acquired. The results can include an increase in bedwetting, a decrease in language, and intensified separation anxiety. These symptoms may negatively affect children's social interactions with peers and adults as well as their adaptation to their first school experience. Very young children rely strongly on adults to protect them from danger, to make the world predictable and safe, and to guide their responses to novel and threatening situations. In the face of violence and terror, the ability of parents, teachers, and other caregivers to provide stability may be negatively affected by their own feelings of helplessness, fear, and grief.

Children 6 to 11. Children in this age group may show extreme withdrawal, depression, anxiety, feelings of guilt, and emotional numbing or "flatness" following exposure to violence. Regressive behaviors at this age include nightmares, sleep problems, irrational fears, and refusal to attend school. Children also may complain of stomachaches or other bodily symptoms that have no medical basis. Children's ability to maintain attention after experiencing violence—either as a witness or a victim—is impeded, often by intrusive images or thoughts related to the violence, causing schoolwork to suffer. Outbursts of anger and fighting and disruptive behavior are also common in traumatized children of this age.

Adolescents. Older children may exhibit responses to terror and violence similar to those of adults, including flashbacks, nightmares, emotional numbing, avoidance of any reminders of the traumatic event, depression, substance abuse, problems with peers, and antisocial behavior. Also common are withdrawal and isolation, physical complaints, suicidal thoughts, school avoidance, academic decline, sleep disturbances, and confusion. The task of developing a stable, coherent, and independent identity is foremost among the tasks of adolescence. Violence or terror can delay or impede the ability of adolescents to gain self-confidence and a clearly formed self-identity.

Refugee and Immigrant Children. Refugee and immigrant children experienced all of the same emotional impacts that American-born children struggled with after September 11. But children (as well as adults) who came to the United States from other countries experienced additional traumas. Many refugees and immigrants came to the United States because of violence in their country of origin. These new arrivals came to the United States with a vision of this country as a permanent respite and haven from the violence, the bloodshed, and the risk of injury and death that they had so recently experienced. September 11 changed that vision, perhaps forever. As one recent refugee put it,

> I experienced the horrors of war in Somalia, and I have prayed that all of this would go away when I came to the United States. Since September 11, it is like being at war all over again.

Cognitive Consequences

A terrorist act, like other kinds of witnessed violence, can challenge a child's understanding of the meaning and purpose of life. Children have less well-developed cognitive skills to make sense of the world and to put troubling events in context than do adults, as the following anecdote illustrates:

> On the day following September 11, Davon, an 8-year-old with Attention Deficit Hyperactivity Disorder, burst into Dr. Anthony's office, trailed by his mother, for a follow-up visit. Davon was having difficulty at school, finding it hard to sit still, to refrain from talking to his friends, and to finish his work. His teacher was constantly reminding him to stay on task. He immediately homed in on two small airplanes in Dr. Anthony's office toy collection and began to "fly" them again and again into the side of his coffee cup, accompanied by crashing noises. His mother reported that he had been watching the television coverage of the attacks steadily over the last day. Dr. Anthony talked with Davon about the events and then asked him why he thought the pilots had flown the planes into the towers. Davon stopped his play and thought for a moment, then quietly said, "They weren't paying attention."

Making sense of horrific events like September 11 is challenging for adults and even more so for children. Children have not had the time to build a solid framework of meaning that would help them explain traumatic events. Many develop illogical or "magical" explanations to cope with seemingly "unexplainable" acts of violence; such explanations should not be dismissed. Instead, teachers and other caregivers should slowly seek to help children incorporate more factually accurate information into their explanations.

What Determines the Impact?

Whether the source is real life or television, it does not take a great deal of violence and terror to threaten a child's sense of security.

Even in the most violent areas—Sarajevo or the Middle East, for instance—shooting, bombing, and killing are intermittent. In many urban neighborhoods, it only takes shots fired once or twice per month and homicides a few times a year to create a year-round climate of danger. One catastrophic terrorist act can destroy a sense of security throughout an entire nation. Memories of the emotions of trauma do not decay; they remain fresh. Once the feeling of danger takes hold, it takes only a small new threat to sustain and even intensify it. In general, the more intense or more frequent are the events, the more a child may experience persistent high levels of distress that disrupt his or her efforts in age-appropriate academic and social pursuits.

For reasons we do not fully understand, some youngsters are more vulnerable to trauma than others. The impact of a traumatic event is likely to be greatest in the child or adolescent who previously has been the victim of child abuse or some other form of trauma, or who already has a mental health problem.

Bias, Prejudice, and Violence Toward Muslims

Soon after September 11, Muslim students and students who were mistakenly targeted as Muslims began experiencing bias, prejudice, harassment, and even violence, both within and outside of school. In a report entitled "After 9/11: Understanding the Impact on Muslim Communities in Maine," the Center for the Prevention of Hate Violence detailed the experience of Muslims after September 11. The report was principally based on interviews with refugees and immigrants conducted by Muslims employed as outreach coordinators by the center.

Our interviews detailed a disturbingly large number of incidents of bias, harassment, threats, and violence toward both adults and students occurring during the nine months following September 11, 2001. The following are some examples:

- Shortly after September 11, two men jumped out of a car and beat up two Muslim boys on their way home from school.

- Two Muslim women were waiting at the bus stop to pick up their children at the end of the school day. While they were waiting, they were spat at and sworn at and told to go back home. Both of the women were wearing *hijabs* (the traditional head covering worn by many Muslim women) as well as other traditional clothing. Since the incident, the two women no longer wait for their children at the bus stop.

- A Muslim high school student missed several days of school after September 11 because she was afraid of being attacked. She wears a hijab and believes that she is a likely target for anger and retaliation. She has not gone anywhere alone since September 11.

- One student recalled: "After September 11, I was made fun of by many people in school. I was threatened by one student twice, and I became afraid to go to school. After September 11, my whole family started to lock doors at our home and always made sure that they locked them at night . . . . I felt like I was trapped in a cage because I was afraid I was going to get hurt, and I really didn't want to go out of my home."

Students at schools both with and without significant populations of Muslim students report the widespread use following September 11 of anti-Muslim slurs and of assertions that *all* Muslims are terrorists. The school experience of many Muslim students has been defined by the fear of the next insult or slur and of the possible escalation to physical violence.

In the interviews we conducted with Muslims and others mistakenly targeted as Muslim, we learned of two additional sources of anxiety and fear. First, many Muslims, both adults and students, reported an intense fear of the possibility of another terrorist attack in the United States attributed to Muslims. This anxiety was directed not only toward the risk of injury or death to family members or friends from such an attack but also toward a renewed and intensified anti-Muslim sentiment that they feared could sweep the country. Second, in significant part as a result of the intensified focus on Muslims by federal law enforcement and immigration officials following September 11, many Muslims are fearful that they will be deported from the United States. This fear is magnified for those Muslims who left their countries because of violence and civil strife. As one refugee put it:

> As refugees, our biggest fear is that we may be deported from the country even though we have not committed any crimes and have legal paperwork. Our fear of having to pack our bags and leave the United States is real. We have already experienced the discomfort of having to leave our home of birth, and we cannot face having to leave our second home in the United States, especially when that home has felt so welcoming.

What We Can Do

As educators, we are not able to eliminate the risk that the United States may experience more serious incidents of terrorism. Moreover, despite a wide variety of efforts to reduce the level of violence in our society, too many children are exposed to traumatizing events as victims or as observers. But we *can* act to help our children by learning to appreciate the profound effect these incidents have on children and to take steps to reduce the associated emotional trauma.

Responding to Future Terrorist Incidents

Talking to Our Children. After a violent event or a disaster occurs, parents, teachers, and other caring adults are the first-line resource for helping young people. We need to reach out to our children to help them deal with the psychological consequences of terror and violence. It is important to remember to use words and concepts that are appropriate for the child's age. Here are some specific suggestions:

• If the terrorist or violent act occurs in close proximity, act first to protect children. Find ways to prevent further exposure to traumatic stimuli. If possible, create a safe haven for children. Protect them from onlookers and the media covering the story. Use a supportive and compassionate verbal or nonverbal exchange (such as a hug, if appropriate) with the child to help him or her feel safe. However brief the exchange, or however temporary, such reassurances are important to children. Identify children in acute distress, which includes panic (marked by trembling, agitation, rambling speech, becoming mute, or erratic behavior) and intense grief (indicated by loud crying, rage, or immobility). Stay with them until they calm down.

• Explain the episode of violence or terror as well as you can. Negative responses to trauma arise when children cannot give meaning to dangerous experiences. Reassure children and adolescents that the traumatic event was not their fault. Children try to understand why such terrible things happen. They call on the lessons taught and modeled at home and school as well as on spiritual values. Traumatic events might initially weaken such beliefs. By continuing to express their moral beliefs and their faith in the predictability of life, adults can work to shore up these supports.

• Encourage children to express their feelings. Listen without passing judgment. Avoidance is often a core part of severe responses to traumatic events; sometimes it can involve avoidance in talking about the event. It is beneficial for children to have the opportunity to talk about violence with caring adults. Help younger children learn to use words that express their feelings. They may often "play with their fears" (for example, pretending to be police officers who rescue those who have been hurt and take them to the hospital to get well). Do not criticize regressive behavior or shame the child with words like "babyish." However, do not force discussion of the traumatic event. Listen and take the lead from the child. Some children may not discuss their experiences with violence because such violence has become somewhat commonplace in their lives. Apathy and desensitization to violence are common reactions among both children and parents.

- Normalize feelings. Let children and adolescents know that it is normal to feel upset after something bad happens. Allow them to be sad; do not expect them to be "brave" or "tough."

- Expect long-term effects. Sometimes adults are concerned that continued attention to terrorist and violent acts is unnecessary and only prolongs recovery. Adults often underestimate the amount of exposure children have had to violence, as well as the impact of that exposure. A gradual return to routines can be reassuring to children; however, it is important to keep checking on their well-being. Effects often emerge after some time has passed. Most children and adolescents, if given support, will recover almost completely from the fear and anxiety caused by a traumatic experience within a few weeks. However, some children and adolescents will need more help, perhaps over a longer period of time, in order to heal. Grief over the loss of someone the child knows may take months to resolve and may be reawakened by reminders such as media reports or the anniversary of the event.

- Encourage children and adolescents to feel in control. Let them make some decisions about meals, what to wear, and similar choices about activities of daily life.

- Reassure. Messages of safety are particularly important in establishing adults as sources of protection and counters to traumatic events. If children are fearful, reassure them that you care for them and will safeguard them. Parents should be advised to increase family activities. Also, parents may wish to alter bedtime procedures. They may be advised to give extra time and reassurance and to let children sleep with a light on or in the parents' room for a limited time if necessary.

How Educators Can Help. A great deal of research highlights the power of parents and teachers in buffering young children from traumatic encounters. Children often measure the danger that threatens them chiefly by the reactions of the trusted adults around them. Security is vitally important for a child's well-being; when children feel safe, they relax and feel comfortable in exploring their environment.

When violence or disaster affects a whole school or community, teachers and school administrators can play a major role in the healing process. Some of the things educators can do are the following:

• Take care of yourself. It is very important for adults to recognize their own responses to violence and terrorist acts. The process of helping youth can be impeded by teachers' own feelings of hopelessness and immobilization. We need to take care of ourselves so we can take care of our children.

• Be alert to the effects of violence. Teachers and other caregivers sometimes may not appreciate children's distress after exposure to violence. Some behaviors of children may not be recognized as effects of trauma. For instance, children who have become excessively concerned about danger may engage in overly aggressive play or experience difficulties in concentration.

• Do not try to rush back to ordinary school routines too soon. Give children or adolescents time to talk over the traumatic event and to express their feelings about it.

• Respect children's preferences. Some children will not want to participate in class discussions about the traumatic event. For these children, referral to a school counselor or other mental health professional may be appropriate.

• Hold in-school sessions with entire classes and with smaller groups of students. These sessions can be very useful in letting students know that their fears and concerns are normal reactions. During these sessions, children can be taught and encouraged to use age-appropriate coping and problem-solving skills to manage anxiety.

• Be sensitive to cultural differences. In some cultures, for example, it is not acceptable to express negative emotions. Children who are reluctant to make eye contact with a teacher may not be depressed, but may simply be exhibiting behavior appropriate to their culture.

• Hold meetings for parents. We know that parents play a key role in helping children to deal with violence. However, parents often are confused about the appropriate ways to talk to their children about terror or other violent acts. Therefore, schools should develop programs to reach out to parents to discuss the traumatic events, their children's response to it, and how they and you can help. Involve mental health professionals in these meetings if possible.

• Refer those with long-lasting effects to other sources of help. In the immediate aftermath of a traumatic event and in the weeks following, it is important to identify the youngsters who are in need of more intensive support and therapy because of profound grief or some other extreme emotion. Children and adolescents who may require the help of a mental health professional include those who show avoidance behavior, such as resisting or refusing to go to places that remind them of the place where the traumatic event occurred, and emotional numbing, a diminished emotional response or lack of feeling toward the event.

Mobilizing Our Students. Teachers, counselors, and administrators can work to empower students to take proactive steps to address the impact of terrorist or other violent incidents. Students can send cards or letters to victims, raise funds to send to organizations that are providing relief and support to the victims of terrorist tragedies, write letters to the editor of local newspapers, and take part in countless other creative activities.

Cumulatively, student efforts at school or after school can make a tangible and important contribution to the nation's efforts to respond to the destruction caused by acts of terror. But these efforts accomplish more than is contained within letters of sympathy sent to families and within envelopes filled with coins sent to relief organizations. These efforts give children a sense of purpose, a sense of control, and a sense that they can make a difference in the face of a world that may seem both cruel and out of control.

Responding to Anti-Muslim Bias and Prejudice

Interrupting Degrading Language. Degrading comments directed at Muslim students, if uninterrupted, can lead to the escalation from slurs to threats to violence. Additionally, the routine use of this type of degrading language can create an intimidating and even terrifying atmosphere for Muslim students and for students who are mistakenly targeted as Muslim. All adults within schools need to be vigilant in interrupting the use of this kind of language, whether or not it is directed at a particular student. Faculty members need to clearly and firmly explain to students that this type of language is degrading, is personally objectionable, and has no place within the school.

Many degrading comments directed at Muslims not only reflect bias and prejudice, but also reflect a fundamental illogic: namely, that if the terrorists associated with September 11 were Muslim, then all Muslims must be terrorists. Teachers need to consistently challenge this biased and unreasoned assumption. Faculty need to explain that there are millions of Muslims in the United States who are not terrorists but rather are our classmates, our neighbors, our physicians, our local storeowners, our teachers, and more.

Educating Our Students About Islam and Muslims. In many schools in the United States in the weeks following September 11, teachers and administrators worked to educate students about the Muslim culture and the religion of Islam. Teachers can present information on Muslim history, culture, and religion as part of classroom curricula. Additionally, many schools have presented programs in which members of the Muslim community have talked about their traditions and educated students about the nature of Islam. These efforts need to continue.

Our Deepest Fear

Unless teachers interrupt degrading comments and slurs directed at Muslims, unless teachers challenge the mistaken and biased assumption that all Muslims are terrorists and present a danger to the United States, and unless we educate our students about the Muslim history, culture, and religion, we may see a perpetuation of anti-Muslim bias and even hate crimes. Moreover, if we do not act, we risk seeing a greatly intensified level of bias, harassment, and intimidation in response to other terrorist attacks that may be attributed to Muslims.

A generation ago, the United States responded to the Japanese attack on Pearl Harbor with fear and prejudice that resulted in the forced relocation and internment of tens of thousands of Japanese American citizens. Fifty years after those events, Americans look back with shame on their treatment of their fellow citizens of Japanese heritage. Our deepest fear is that the next generation of students may read in their social studies textbooks of the shameful treatment of Arab Americans and other Muslim Americans after the events of September 11. That history has not yet been written— at least not completely. That history need not be written. As educators, we have the opportunity and the ability to create a climate within our schools in which students of all religions and nationalities and ethnicities are respected, and in which students of any one religion, nationality, or ethnicity are not unfairly stereotyped and blamed for the horrific and tragic deeds of a few. If our children treat each other with this kind of respect, we can hope that the adults in their lives will do the same.

References

Center for the Prevention of Hate Violence. (2002). After 9/11: Understanding the impact on Muslim communities in Maine. Available at www.cphv.usm.maine.edu.

Cicchetti, D., & Toth, S. L. (1997). *Rochester symposium on developmental psychopathology: Vol. 8, Developmental perspectives on trauma: Theory, research, and intervention*. Rochester, NY: University of Rochester Press.

Marans, S., & Adelman, A. (1997). Experiencing violence in a developmental context. In J. D. Osofsky (Ed.), *Children in a violent society* (pp. 202–222). New York: Guilford Press.

Margolin, G., & Gordis, C. B. (2000). The effects of family and community violence on children. *Annual Review of Psychology, 51*, 445–479.

Schuster, M. A., Stein, B. D., Jaycox, L. A., Collins, R. L., Marshall, G. N., Elliott, M. N., Zhou, A. J., Kanouse, D. E., Morrison, J. L., & Berry, S. H. (2001). A national survey of stress reactions after the September 11, 2001, terrorist attacks. *New England Journal of Medicine, 345*, 1507–1512.

9

STANDING UP FOR EACH OTHER

Recently the Center for the Prevention of Hate Violence presented a program on preventing harassment to more than 150 high school students participating in the Upward Bound program. After I spoke for about 30 minutes on issues of bias, prejudice, and harassment, the students broke into small groups facilitated by staff members. They discussed their own experiences with bias and harassment in their schools—and most important, what they could do to make their Upward Bound experience as safe and respectful as possible. After the program, several students and staff members stayed to talk. While we were talking, I noticed two boys waiting, standing several feet apart. Eventually one of the two asked if he could talk to me.

The boy, a junior from a small high school, proceeded to describe harassment he had endured that started in *3rd grade*. After 10 minutes, when he was relating incidents that had occurred in 4th grade, I broke in to ask whether the harassment was still continuing. He told me that the harassment was still a big problem and immediately returned to finish his description of his 4th grade year. Soon I helped him to focus on the current situation in his school and what he could do about it. But I realized that this boy evidently has been suffering humiliation, degradation, and some amount of physical violence for virtually his entire school life. At some point, he turned to the Upward Bound director and said, "This is the first time I have ever been in a school experience where I have not been afraid. It has never happened before." He began to cry and came to me to both give and receive a warm hug.

The first boy then stepped aside to let the second boy speak with me. The second boy, also a high school junior, began to describe his own experiences with harassment beginning in 1st grade. He also described a continuing series of degrading and humiliating encounters with other students over the past 10 years. He too began to cry. I asked the second boy if he could think of one adult in his school to whom he could talk about the harassment. He shook his head through his tears. As he composed himself, I asked him to think carefully. Was there even one person—a teacher, an administrator, a coach, a counselor—to whom he could talk about his situation? He looked at me with tears in his eyes and said, "I can't think of anybody who cares." Both boys then turned to leave. As they walked out of the auditorium, I saw the first boy put his arm around the second.

The pain felt by these boys was terribly real. Sadly, it probably is very deep and lasting. I am certain that both boys had teachers, administrators, counselors, and others in their school who do care about harassment; these adults would be upset to learn that even one student felt there was no one to look to for help. We can—we *must*—create schools in which adults send messages to students that harassment is wrong, that harassment is not tolerated, and that those students who are harassed have many individuals to turn to for help.

We *can* create schools in which no child must suffer day after day, week after week, month after month, and year after year a life of loneliness, degradation, and despair. We can create these kinds of schools, but only if we demonstrate leadership—only if we stand up and speak up for civility and respect. We can create schools where every single child feels respected and valued, but only if administrators provide vocal and ongoing leadership. Administrators must take the lead in emphasizing the need for everyone to treat one another with respect and in providing resources that enable both faculty and students to develop the understanding and tools to prevent and respond to harassment.

We can create these kinds of respectful schools only when faculty members interrupt the routine use of degrading language in the hallways, in the lunchroom, in the locker room, and elsewhere within the school community. Our teachers are critical role models for respect and civility, both within and outside of the classroom.

Finally, we can change our schools only when we empower students to assume responsibility for the harassment that is perpetrated on their classmates. The capacity of our young people to act courageously and with passion is almost limitless.

*   *   *

In my work in schools, I have met many people who have shown tremendous courage. They have included principals, teachers, coaches, guidance counselors, and students. It is fitting to close this book with a story of courage.

Several years ago, on an early Friday evening in mid-June, nine high school 9th graders decided to walk from their small rural town to a nearby swimming hole. The nine boys were walking down a dirt road about a mile outside of town when they heard a car coming toward them. In the car they saw four young men, 19 through 22. One of the four men yelled a racial slur about black people. One of the nine boys was black; the others were white. The black student was the only student of color in the entire high school.

The car continued 50 or 60 feet past the nine friends and then, skidding and churning up dust, turned around. As the car came toward the nine teenagers for a second time, one of the passengers yelled the same racial slur while dangling a sturdy rope tied in a noose out the window. Again the car drove past the students. Again it turned, spitting up dust, to come back toward them. This time, however, the car skidded to a stop a dozen feet from the nine friends.

The driver of the car stared intently at the black student, yelled a racial slur, hung the noose out of the car window, and said, "You come over here." The sole black student was momentarily paralyzed. He could not believe this was happening to him, and he did not know what to do. Then he took one half step forward as if he was going to walk to the car.

At that point, something remarkable occurred. The boy standing next to him, without looking at his classmate, put his right arm across the chest of his friend to stop him from going to the car. With his eyes fixed on the driver of the car, he said in a strong and measured voice, "If he comes, we all come. Because we stick together." There was absolute silence for seven or eight seconds. Then the coward behind the wheel of that car did what cowards usually do when somebody stands up to them. He put his right foot on the accelerator and the car sped off.

Four years later, I spoke to the incoming first-year class at a large state university on the first day that students were on campus. I closed my remarks by relating this story. As I was preparing to leave the auditorium, a young man walked toward me. He approached me and said, "I just wanted to let you know that I was one of those nine students." I asked him how he was feeling; he said, "I'm feeling pretty chilled right now." After a very long pause he said, "You know, I really miss my friends."

The courage of those nine high school freshmen was the only thing that prevented disaster. If they had not stood up for one another, this small town in rural Maine could easily have become as infamous as Laramie, Wyoming—where Matthew Shepard, a gay college student, was beaten mercilessly and then tied to a fence post to die—or Jasper, Texas—where James Byrd Jr., a black man, was dragged behind a pickup truck until his head was severed from his body.

When our young people finish their school experience, they will—we hope—have attained the benefits of an education. They will use the substantive knowledge and skills learned in classrooms and extracurricular activities throughout the rest of their lives. But our young people will also rely on what they learned individually and as a group about the value of looking out for each other.

After the tragedy at Columbine High School, students throughout the country heard experts (many of whom, it seemed, had not been inside a high school since their own graduation) rail against the culture of disrespect and violence among teenagers. Students also witnessed the response of many school administrators who dramatically increased security measures, including the use of video cameras and metal detectors. The message received by students was clear: the problem of disrespect and violence in schools is the result of this generation of teenagers.

But I have reached a different conclusion, based on my experience with peer leader projects and countless conversations with student leaders in schools nationwide. As a society, we must undertake a shift in our thinking. The problem of violence and disrespect in schools is *not* teenagers. Instead, the *solutions* to these problems are our students! I have no doubt that the nation's single most powerful resource in addressing problems of civility and bias is those countless young people who have the empathy and the courage to speak up for respect.

The courage and compassion of young people are a virtually limitless tool for creating safe and respectful environments for our children's living and learning. Our task—as administrators, as teachers, as counselors, as coaches, as parents, and as friends to young people—is to model the confidence and courage to stand up for civility and respect and to provide the time and the resources to allow our young people to develop that courage that exists within all of us.

Appendix

Organizations and Web Sites

This list of resources is intended to provide educators with a starting point for next steps. In addition to those included here, many other valuable resources on preventing bias, harassment, and violence are currently available to educators.

Anti-Defamation League

823 UN Plaza
New York, NY 10017
Phone: 212-490-2525
www.adl.org

ADL is a not-for-profit civil rights and human relations organization dedicated to combating anti-Semitism and bigotry of all kinds, defending democratic ideals, and safeguarding civil rights.

A World of Difference Institute

Anti-Defamation League
National Headquarters
Phone: 212-885-7700
E-mail: webmaster@adl.org
www.adl.org

The institute provides training and curriculum used by schools, universities, corporations, and law enforcement agencies to challenge prejudice and discrimination. The goals of the institute include recognizing bias and the harm it inflicts on individuals and society, exploring the value of diversity, improving intergroup relations, and combating racism, anti-Semitism, and all forms of prejudice and bigotry. The institute has a number of valuable publications available through its Web site.

Center for the Prevention of Hate Violence

University of Southern Maine
96 Falmouth Street, Box 9300
Portland, ME 04104
Phone: 207-780-4756
www.cphv.usm.maine.edu

CPHV develops and implements programs to prevent bias, harassment, and violence, and helps schools, colleges, law enforcement agencies, and communities to respond to hate crimes. CPHV provides training and workshops for students, educators (K–12 and college), law enforcement professionals, health care and mental health care professionals, and community members.

Children's Defense Fund

25 E Street, NW
Washington, DC 20001
Phone: 202-628-8787
www.childrensdefense.org

CDF provides a strong, effective voice for *all* children in the United States. CDF educates the nation about the needs of children and encourages preventive investment before children become ill, drop out of school, or suffer family breakdown. CDF provides resources and programs for teachers, students, and parents.

Facing History and Ourselves

16 Hurd Road
Brookline, MA 02445
Phone: 617-232-1595
www.facing.org

Facing History and Ourselves is a nonprofit educational organization that works with middle and high school teachers, students, and communities to examine racism, prejudice, and anti-Semitism through the study of the historical development of the Holocaust and other examples of collective violence.

Gay, Lesbian and Straight Education Network

121 West 27th Street
Suite 804
New York, NY 10001
Phone: 212-727-0254
www.glsen.org

GLSEN believes that the key to ending antigay prejudice and hate-motivated violence is education. GLSEN provides online staff development resources and curriculum for K–12 teachers relating to lesbian, gay, bisexual, and transgender issues and information on how teachers can make school a safe and supportive environment for all students.

Leadership Education for Asian Pacifics, Inc.

327 East 2nd Street
Suite 226
Los Angeles, CA 90012
Phone: 213-485-1422
www.leap.org

LEAP is a national nonprofit organization working to achieve full participation and equality for Asian Pacific Americans. LEAP offers leadership training, publishes original public policy research, and conducts community education to advance a comprehensive strategy for the empowerment of Asian Pacific Americans.

Leadership Conference Education Fund

1629 K Street, NW
Suite 1010
Washington, DC 20006
www.civilrights.org

LCEF works to combat discrimination in all its forms and seeks to build the public understanding that is essential for the United States to continue its journey toward social and economic justice. LCEF develops print and Web-based resources for teachers, students, and community members.

NAACP

4805 Mt. Hope Drive
Baltimore, MD 21215
Toll Free: 877-NAACP-98
24-Hour Hotline: 410-521-4939
www.naacp.org

The primary focus of the NAACP is the protection and enhancement of the civil rights of African Americans and other minorities. The fundamental goal of the NAACP's education advocacy agenda is to provide all students access to quality education. The NAACP seeks to accomplish this goal through policy development, training, collaboration, negotiation, legislation, litigation, and agitation.

National Conference for Community and Justice

475 Park Avenue South
19th Floor
New York, NY 10016
Phone: 212-545-1300
www.nccj.org

NCCJ is a human relations organization dedicated to fighting bias, bigotry, and racism in the United States. NCCJ promotes understanding and respect among all races, religions, and cultures through advocacy, conflict resolution, and educational programs.

National Congress of American Indians

1301 Connecticut Avenue, NW
Washington, DC 20036
Phone: 202-466-7767
www.ncai.org

NCAI works to inform the public and Congress on the rights of American Indians and Alaska Natives. Current issues and activities of the NCAI include protection of programs and services benefiting Indian families and promotion and support of Indian education.

National Council of La Raza

1111 19th Street, NW
Suite 1000
Washington, DC 20036
Phone: 202-785-1670
www.nclr.org

The National Council of La Raza works to reduce poverty and discrimination, and to improve life opportunities for Hispanic Americans. The council provides information for teachers and community members on building community-school education collaboratives, strengthening the quality of education for Hispanic students, and on ways to effectively involve Hispanic families in the education of their children.

Office of Juvenile Justice and Delinquency Prevention

810 Seventh Street, NW
Washington, DC 20531
Phone: 202-307-5911
http://ojjdp.ncjrs.org

OJJDP provides programs, publications, and other resources for educators and communities on a broad range of topics relating to youth violence prevention. OJJDP has a number of valuable publications available through its Web site.

Partners Against Hate

1100 Connecticut Avenue, NW
Suite 1020
Washington, DC 20036
Phone: 202-452-8310
www.partnersagainsthate.org

Partners Against Hate is a joint effort of the Anti-Defamation League, the Leadership Conference Education Fund, and the Center for the Prevention of Hate Violence to design and implement a program of outreach, public education, and training. Partners Against Hate provides strategies and resources for trainers, parents and families, law enforcement agencies, educators, and youth, community, and business leaders to improve knowledge and response to youth-initiated hate violence. Partners Against Hate has a number of valuable publications available through its Web site. Partners Against Hate conducts regional trainer conferences to prepare two-person teams (consisting of a police officer and an educator) to present antiharassment peer leader and faculty training.

Safe and Drug-Free Schools Program

United States Department of Education
Phone: 202-260-3954
www.ed.gov/offices/OESE/SDFS/index.html

The Safe and Drug-Free Schools Program works to reduce drug, alcohol, and tobacco use and violence through education and prevention activities in U.S. schools.

The Simon Wiesenthal Center

1399 South Roxbury Drive
Los Angeles, CA 90035
Phone: 310-553-9036
800-900-9036 (toll-free from within the United States)
www.wiesenthal.com

The Simon Wiesenthal Center is a human rights organization dedicated to preserving the memory of the Holocaust by fostering tolerance and understanding. The center provides training for educators and police officers.

The Southern Poverty Law Center

400 Washington Avenue
Montgomery, AL 36104
334-956-8200
www.splcenter.org

SPLC is a nonprofit organization that combats hate, intolerance, and discrimination through education and litigation. SPLC provides resources for teachers, parents, and students.

Teaching Tolerance

c/o The Southern Poverty Law Center
400 Washington Avenue
Montgomery, AL 36104
http://tolerance.org/teach/index.jsp

Teaching Tolerance is a program of the Southern Poverty Law Center and is an online resource that provides teaching materials, professional development resources, and a forum for connecting with other teachers, parents, and students.

INDEX

ABOUT THE AUTHOR

Stephen L. Wessler is the Director of the Center for the Prevention of Hate Violence at the University of Southern Maine, where he is also a research associate professor with the College of Arts and Sciences and the Muskie School of Public Service. The center develops and implements programs in schools, colleges, and communities to prevent bias, prejudice, harassment, and violence, and promotes writing and teaching on issues relating to bias-motivated violence.

Wessler, an attorney, developed and directed the civil rights enforcement effort at the Maine Department of the Attorney General from 1992 to 1999. In 1996, he developed with a colleague the Civil Rights Team Project, a hate violence prevention program conducted by the Attorney General's Office, which is now in more than 200 Maine middle and high schools. Wessler has conducted scores of trainings on preventing hate violence to educators, students, police officers, and community members. In 1998, he participated in the U.S. Department of Justice's Working Group, which developed and piloted the National Hate Crimes Training Curriculum.

Wessler is a graduate of Harvard College and Boston University School of Law. He practiced law both in the Attorney General's Office and in private practice for more than 22 years before creating the Center for the Prevention of Hate Violence in 1999. Wessler also has received recognitions or awards for his work in civil rights from the Maine Lesbian and Gay Political Alliance (1993), the Portland Branch of the NAACP (1994), the Jewish Federation of Southern Maine (1994), the Maine Civil Liberties Union (1996), the Maine Children's Alliance (1997), the Maine Education Association (1997), GLAD (Gay & Lesbian Advocates and Defenders) (1999), The Association of Educational Publishers (Distinguished Achievement Award for article published in *Educational Leadership*, June 2001), and Maine Bar Foundation (Howard Dana Award, 2002, for services provided to Maine's vulnerable populations).

Related ASCD Resources: The Respectful School: How Educators and Students Can Conquer Hate and Harassment

At the time of publication, the following ASCD resources were available; for the most up-to-date information about ASCD resources, go to www.ascd.org. ASCD stock numbers are noted in parentheses.

Audiotapes

Beyond Bullying by Beth Madison (#203153) **Also on CD!**

Community in School: The Neglected Dimension of Reform by Eric Schaps, Larry Leverett, Kristie Finh, Michele Alterlind Brynjulson (#203203) **Also on CD!**

Helping Schools Respond to Terrorism and Other Traumatic Events by Steve Sroka (#203199) **Also on CD!**

Improving Student Learning and Safety: The Character and Conduct Approach by Francine Banyon, Richard Banyon, Roberta Richin, and Rita Prager Stein (#201113)

Leadership for Teaching Tolerance in Our Schools by Ting-Yi Oei (#203077)

Solutions for Preventing Violence, Reducing Suspensions, and Promoting Positive School Behavior by James Lawrence (#200082)

Multimedia

Quick Response: A Step-by-Step Guide to Crisis Management for Principals, Counselors and Teachers (topic pack) (#197175)

Networks

Visit the ASCD Web site (www.ascd.org) and search for "networks" for information about professional educators who have formed groups around topics like "Gay, Lesbian, Bisexual, Transgendered and Allied Issues in Education Network," and "Hispanic/Latino American Critical Issues." Look in the "Network Directory" for current facilitators' addresses and phone numbers.

Online Resources

Visit ASCD's Web site (www.ascd.org) for the following professional development opportunities:

Online Tutorial: *School Safety* (free)
Professional Development Online: *Conflict Resolution* and *Embracing Diversity, Respecting Others*, among others (for a small fee; password protected).

Print Products

Educational Leadership: Creating Caring Schools (entire issue, March 2003) Excerpted articles online free; entire issue online and accessible to ASCD members

Reducing School Violence Through Conflict Resolution by David Johnson and Roger Johnson (#195198)

The Soul of Education: Helping Students Find Connection, Compassion, and Character at School by Rachael Kessler (#100045)

As Tough as Necessary: Countering Violence, Aggression, and Hostility in Our Schools by Richard L. Curwin and Allen N. Mendler (#197017)

Videos

A Safe Place to Learn: Crisis Response and School Safety Planning (One videotape with *Facilitator's Guide* and the book *How to Prepare and Respond to a Crisis* by John J. Schonfeld, Robert Lictenstein, Marsha Kline Pruett, and Dee Speese-Linehan (#496062)

Teacher as Community Builder (Tape 3 of *The Teacher Series*) (#401084)

For more information, visit us on the World Wide Web (http://www.ascd.org), send an e-mail message to member@ascd.org, call the ASCD Service Center (1-800-933-ASCD or 703-578-9600, then press 2), send a fax to 703-575-5400, or write to Information Services, ASCD, 1703 N. Beauregard St., Alexandria, VA 22311-1714 USA.